Better Homes and Gardens®

fast &
fresh
family dinners

Better Homes and Gardens®

fast &
fresh
family dinners

JG
PRESS

Published by World Publications Group, Inc., 140 Laurel Street, East Bridgewater, MA 02333, www.wrldpub.net

Library of Congress Cataloging-in-Publication Data:

Fast & fresh family dinners.
    p. cm.
  Parallel title: At head of title: Better homes and gardens
  Includes index.
  ISBN 978-1-57215-626-5 (cloth) -- ISBN 978-1-57215-631-9 (pbk.)
  1. Quick and easy cookery. 2. Dinners and dining. I. Better homes and gardens. II. Title: Better homes and gardens fast & fresh family dinners. III. Title: Better homes and gardens.
  TX833..F38 2010
  641.5'55--dc22

2010019517

Printed in China.

10 9 8 7 6 5 4 3 2 1

Test Kitchen

Our seal assures you that every recipe in *Fast & Fresh Family Dinners* has been tested in the Better Homes and Gardens Test Kitchen®. This means that each recipe is practical and reliable and meets our high standards of taste appeal. We guarantee your satisfaction with this book for as long as you own it.

contents

20-minute MEALS

Shrimp Quesadillas, *recipe page 26*

salsa, BEAN, AND CHEESE PIZZA

Start to Finish: 20 minutes
Oven: 425°F
Makes: 4 servings

4   **6-inch corn tortillas***
4   **teaspoons olive oil**
1   **medium onion, chopped
    (½ cup)**
1   **fresh jalapeño chile pepper,
    seeded and finely chopped
    (see tip)***
1   **clove garlic, minced**
1   **cup rinsed and drained
    canned black beans**
1   **cup chopped, seeded tomato**
4   **ounces Monterey Jack,
    cheddar, or mozzarella
    cheese, shredded (1 cup)**
2   **tablespoons chopped fresh
    cilantro**

① Preheat the oven to 425°F. Place tortillas on an ungreased baking sheet. Lightly brush tortillas on both sides with 1 teaspoon of the olive oil. Bake for about 3 minutes on each side or until light brown and crisp.

② Meanwhile, in a large skillet, cook onion, chile pepper, and garlic in the remaining 3 teaspoons oil over medium-high heat until onion is tender. Stir in black beans and tomato; heat through.

③ Sprinkle tortillas with half of the cheese. Spoon bean mixture over cheese. Sprinkle with remaining cheese. Bake for about 4 minutes or until cheese melts. Sprinkle with cilantro.

Nutrition facts per serving: 231 cal., 11 g total fat (4 g sat. fat), 20 mg chol., 496 mg sodium, 25 g carbo., 12 g pro.

*Test Kitchen Tips: If you prefer, substitute purchased tostada shells for the corn tortillas; reduce the amount of oil to 3 teaspoons and omit Step 1.

When working with chile peppers, wear plastic or rubber gloves. If your bare hands do touch the peppers, wash your hands and nails well with soap and warm water.

ravioli WITH SPINACH PESTO

Start to Finish: 20 minutes
Makes: 4 servings

- **1 9-ounce package refrigerated four-cheese ravioli or tortellini**
- **12 ounces baby pattypan squash, halved, or yellow summer squash, halved lengthwise and sliced ½ inch thick**
- **3½ cups fresh baby spinach**
- **½ cup torn fresh basil**
- **¼ cup bottled Caesar vinaigrette salad dressing**
- **2 tablespoons water**
- **Shredded Parmesan cheese (optional)**

1 Cook ravioli according to package directions, adding squash for the last 2 minutes of cooking. Drain.

2 Meanwhile, for pesto, in a blender, combine spinach, basil, salad dressing, and the water. Cover and process until smooth, stopping to scrape down blender as needed.

3 Toss ravioli mixture with pesto. If desired, sprinkle with cheese.

Nutrition facts per serving: 218 cal., 6 g total fat (2 g sat. fat), 27 mg chol., 525 mg sodium, 31 g carbo., 11 g pro.

ravioli WITH ZUCCHINI

Start to Finish: 18 minutes
Makes: 4 servings

1 **9-ounce package refrigerated whole wheat cheese-filled ravioli**

½ **cup walnuts, coarsely chopped**

2 **tablespoons olive oil**

2 **medium zucchini, halved lengthwise and sliced**

6 **green onions, diagonally sliced ¼ inch thick**

½ **cup milk**

1 **cup finely shredded Parmesan cheese (4 ounces)**

⅛ **teaspoon salt**

⅛ **teaspoon ground black pepper**

1 Cook ravioli in boiling salted water for 6 to 8 minutes or until tender; drain.

2 Meanwhile, in a large skillet, cook walnuts in hot oil over medium heat for 2 to 3 minutes; remove with a slotted spoon. Add zucchini and green onions to skillet. Cook and stir for 2 to 3 minutes or until vegetables are crisp-tender.

3 Add pasta, walnuts, milk, and ¾ cup of the cheese to the pan. Cook and toss for 1 minute. Season with salt and pepper. Transfer to serving bowls; sprinkle with remaining cheese.

Nutrition facts per serving: 466 cal., 29 g total fat (9 g sat. fat), 59 mg chol., 859 mg sodium, 33 g carbo., 21 g pro.

pasta AND FRESH TOMATO SAUCE

This pasta sauce is the essence of simplicity—chopped Roma tomatoes lightly sautéed in a little olive oil and seasoned with basil. Served on the side, it's the ideal accompaniment to beef, chicken, or seafood.

Start to Finish: 20 minutes
Makes: 4 servings

- **4 ounces dried rotini or fusilli**
- **2 cups coarsely chopped plum tomatoes**
- **2 teaspoons olive oil**
- **¼ teaspoon salt**
- **3 tablespoons shredded fresh basil**
- **¼ cup shaved or grated Parmesan or Romano cheese**
- **¼ teaspoon ground black pepper**

1 Cook the pasta according to package directions; drain.

2 Meanwhile, in a saucepan combine tomatoes, olive oil, and salt. Cook over medium-low heat until heated through and tomatoes start to release their juices slightly. Stir in the basil.

3 Divide pasta among 4 plates. Top each serving with some of the tomato mixture. Sprinkle with Parmesan cheese and pepper.

Nutrition facts per ½ cup pasta and ⅜ cup sauce: 184 cal., 5 g total fat (2 g sat. fat), 5 mg chol., 260 mg sodium, 28 g carbo., 7 g pro.

tortellini AND PEAS

Start to Finish: 20 minutes
Makes: 4 servings

1 9-ounce package refrigerated cheese-filled tortellini or ravioli

1 cup frozen peas

2 tablespoons all-purpose flour

⅛ teaspoon ground black pepper

1 cup half-and-half, light cream, or milk

1 14.5-ounce can diced tomatoes with basil, garlic, and oregano, undrained

Salt

Ground black pepper

2 tablespoons shredded Parmesan cheese

1 Cook tortellini according to package directions, adding peas for the last minute of cooking. Drain. Return tortellini mixture to pan; cover to keep warm.

2 Meanwhile, for sauce, in a medium saucepan, stir together flour and ⅛ teaspoon pepper. Gradually stir in half-and-half. Cook and stir over medium heat until thickened and bubbly. Cook and stir for 1 minute more. Gradually stir in undrained tomatoes. Season with salt and additional pepper.

3 Pour sauce over tortellini mixture; toss gently to coat. Sprinkle with Parmesan cheese.

Nutrition facts per serving: 410 cal., 13 g total fat (7 g sat. fat), 54 mg chol., 998 mg sodium, 57 g carbo., 18 g pro.

hearty ITALIAN STEW

Start to Finish: 15 minutes
Makes: 6 servings

1 teaspoon bottled minced garlic

1 tablespoon olive oil

2 14.5-ounce cans diced tomatoes with basil, garlic, and oregano, undrained

1 14-ounce can beef broth

1¾ cups water

1 16-ounce package frozen cooked Italian-style meatballs

½ of a 16-ounce package frozen yellow, green, and red sweet peppers and onion stir-fry vegetables

1 9-ounce package refrigerated three-cheese tortellini

½ of a 10-ounce package shredded cabbage (about 3 cups)

Grated Parmesan cheese

1. In a 4- to 5-quart Dutch oven, cook garlic in hot oil over medium heat for 30 seconds. Stir in undrained tomatoes, beef broth, and the water. Add meatballs and frozen pepper blend. Bring mixture to boiling over medium-high heat. Stir in tortellini and cabbage. Cook, covered, for 5 minutes more. Ladle stew into bowls; sprinkle with Parmesan cheese.

Nutrition facts per serving: 459 cal., 23 g total fat (10 g sat. fat), 71 mg chol., 1,705 mg sodium, 40 g carbo., 23 g pro.

hamburger-barley SOUP

Prep: 30 minutes
Cook: 20 minutes
Makes: 8 servings

1½ pounds extra-lean ground
beef

2 cups thinly sliced carrot
(4 medium)

1 cup chopped onion (1 large)

1 cup sliced celery (2 stalks)

½ cup chopped green sweet
pepper (1 small)

1 clove garlic, minced

3 14-ounce cans beef broth

1 28-ounce can diced tomatoes

1 8-ounce can tomato sauce

½ cup quick-cooking barley

2 bay leaves

1 teaspoon Worcestershire
sauce

1 teaspoon dried oregano,
crushed, or 1 tablespoon
snipped fresh oregano

¼ teaspoon ground black
pepper

¼ teaspoon salt

Fresh oregano sprigs
(optional)

1 In a 5- to 6-quart Dutch oven, cook beef, carrot, onion, celery, sweet pepper, and garlic over medium heat until meat is brown and vegetables are tender. Drain well; return to Dutch oven.

2 Stir in beef broth. Stir in undrained tomatoes, tomato sauce, barley, bay leaves, Worcestershire sauce, dried or snipped oregano, black pepper, and salt. Bring to boiling; reduce heat. Cover and simmer for about 20 minutes or until barley is tender. Discard bay leaves. If desired, garnish with oregano sprigs.

Nutrition facts per serving: 237 cal., 8 g total fat (3 g sat. fat), 54 mg chol., 990 mg sodium, 20 g carbo., 19 g pro.

southwestern STEAK CHILI

Start to Finish: 20 minutes
Makes: 4 servings

1   cup frozen whole kernel corn, thawed

1   to 1½ teaspoons chili powder

1   tablespoon cooking oil

1   17-ounce package refrigerated cooked beef sirloin tips with gravy

1   16-ounce jar mild or medium thick and chunky salsa

1   14- to 16-ounce can pinto or red beans, rinsed and drained

¼   cup hickory-flavor barbecue sauce

¼   cup dairy sour cream

1 In a large saucepan or Dutch oven, cook corn and chili powder in hot oil over medium heat for 3 minutes, stirring frequently. Stir in beef tips with gravy, salsa, beans, and barbecue sauce. Bring to boiling, stirring occasionally to break up beef slightly. Reduce heat. Simmer, covered, for 5 minutes. Top each serving with a tablespoon of sour cream.

Nutrition facts per serving: 354 cal., 11 g total fat (3 g sat. fat), 47 mg chol., 1,834 mg sodium, 42 g carbo., 25 g pro.

tequila-lime CHICKEN

Start to Finish: 15 minutes
Makes: 4 servings

1   9-ounce package refrigerated
    fettuccine

1   lime

1   10-ounce container
    refrigerated regular or light
    Alfredo sauce

¼   cup tequila or milk

1   9-ounce package refrigerated
    cooked grilled chicken
    breast strips

1 Cook the fettuccine according to package directions; drain. Meanwhile, finely shred enough peel from the lime to equal 1 teaspoon. Cut lime into wedges; set aside.

2 In a medium saucepan, heat and stir Alfredo sauce, peel, and tequila just to boiling. Stir in chicken strips; heat through. Toss sauce with hot fettuccine. Serve with lime wedges.

Nutrition facts per serving: 528 cal., 24 g total fat (1 g sat. fat), 123 mg chol., 853 mg sodium, 39 g carbo., 11 g pro.

pesto PENNE WITH ROASTED CHICKEN

Start to Finish: 20 minutes
Makes: 4 servings

8 ounces dried penne, mostaccioli, or bowtie pasta (4 cups)

2 cups broccoli florets

1 7-ounce container purchased basil pesto

2½ cups bite-size slices purchased roasted chicken or leftover roasted chicken

1 7-ounce jar roasted red sweet peppers, drained and cut into strips

¼ cup finely shredded Parmesan cheese

Finely shredded Parmesan cheese (optional)

½ teaspoon coarsely ground black pepper

1 Cook pasta according to package directions, adding broccoli for the last 2 minutes of cooking. Drain, reserving ½ cup of the pasta water. Return drained pasta and broccoli to the pot.

2 In a small bowl, combine pesto and reserved pasta water. Add chicken, roasted red peppers, and pesto mixture to pasta in pot. Toss gently to coat. Heat through over medium heat. Add ¼ cup Parmesan cheese to pasta mixture and toss to combine.

3 Divide pasta among four warm pasta bowls. If desired, top with additional Parmesan cheese. Sprinkle with black pepper.

Nutrition facts per serving: 672 cal., 35 g total fat (7 g sat. fat), 93 mg chol., 857 mg sodium, 37 g pro.

rosemary CHICKEN
WITH VEGETABLES

Start to Finish: 30 minutes
Makes: 4 servings

4 medium skinless, boneless chicken breast halves

½ teaspoon lemon-pepper seasoning

2 tablespoons olive oil

4 ounces refrigerated spinach or plain linguine

2 cloves garlic, minced

2 medium zucchini and/or yellow summer squash, cut into ¼-inch slices

½ cup apple juice

2 teaspoons snipped fresh rosemary or ½ teaspoon dried rosemary, crushed

2 tablespoons dry white wine or chicken broth

2 teaspoons cornstarch

1 cup halved cherry or grape tomatoes

Fresh rosemary sprigs (optional)

1 Sprinkle chicken with lemon-pepper seasoning. In a large skillet, cook chicken in hot oil over medium heat for 8 to 10 minutes or until chicken is no longer pink, turning once. Transfer chicken to a platter; cover and keep warm. Meanwhile, cook pasta according to package directions; drain and keep warm.

2 Add garlic to skillet; cook for 15 seconds. Add zucchini, apple juice, and rosemary. Bring to boiling; reduce heat. Cover and simmer for 2 minutes.

3 In a small bowl, stir together wine and cornstarch; add to skillet. Cook and stir until thickened and bubbly; cook for 2 minutes more. Stir in tomatoes. Serve vegetables and pasta with chicken. If desired, garnish with rosemary sprigs.

Nutrition facts per serving: 326 cal., 10 g total fat (2 g sat. fat), 95 mg chol., 247 mg sodium, 25 g carbo., 2 g fiber, 33 g pro.

turkey SPINACH TOSS

Start to Finish: 20 minutes
Makes: 4 servings

2 **turkey breast tenderloins, split in half horizontally (about 1 pound)**
   Ground black pepper
2 **tablespoons butter**
2 **ounces thinly sliced deli ham**
½ **cup orange juice**
2 **9- to 10-ounce packages fresh spinach**
1 **orange, cut into wedges**
   Salt

1 Season turkey with ground black pepper. In a very large skillet, cook turkey in hot butter over medium-high heat for 12 minutes or until no longer pink (170°F), turning once. Remove turkey from skillet. Slice into strips; cover and keep warm.

2 Add ham to skillet; cook and stir for 1 minute or until heated and starting to crisp. Remove ham from skillet. Add juice; bring to boiling. Add spinach, half at a time; cook for 1 minute. Add orange wedges with second batch of spinach. Using tongs, remove spinach and oranges from skillet; divide among plates. Sprinkle with salt and pepper. Top with turkey and ham. Drizzle with juices from skillet.

Nutrition facts per serving: 244 cal., 8 g total fat (4 g sat. fat), 94 mg chol., 528 mg sodium, 9 g carbo., 34 g pro.

shrimp QUESADILLAS

Start to Finish: 20 minutes
Makes: 4 servings

4   **8-inch vegetable tortillas**
    Nonstick cooking spray

½   **of a 7-ounce carton garlic or**
    spicy three-pepper hummus
    (⅓ cup)

6   **ounces peeled, deveined**
    cooked shrimp

1   **6-ounce jar marinated**
    artichoke hearts or ½ of a
    16-ounce jar pickled mixed
    vegetables, drained and
    coarsely chopped

1   **4-ounce package crumbled**
    feta cheese

1 Coat one side of each tortilla with nonstick cooking spray. Place tortillas, sprayed side down, on a work surface; spread with hummus. Top half of each tortilla with shrimp, artichokes, and cheese. Fold tortillas in half, pressing gently.

2 Heat a large nonstick skillet or griddle over medium heat for 1 minute. Cook quesadillas, two at a time, for 4 to 6 minutes or until brown and heated through, turning once.

Nutrition facts per serving: 430 cal., 20 g total fat (7 g sat. fat), 108 mg chol., 1,099 mg sodium, 42 g carbo., 21 g pro.

shrimply DIVINE PASTA

Start to Finish: 20 minutes
Makes: 4 servings

1   6-ounce package rotini or other pasta

12 ounces frozen medium shrimp, thawed, peeled, and deveined

3   cloves garlic, minced

1   tablespoon olive oil

1   cup chicken broth

1   tablespoon cornstarch

1   teaspoon dried basil, crushed

1   teaspoon dried oregano, crushed

4   cups prewashed (packaged) baby spinach or torn spinach

    Finely shredded Parmesan cheese

1 Cook pasta according to package directions. Drain well; keep pasta warm.

2 Meanwhile, rinse shrimp; pat dry with paper towels. For sauce, in a large skillet, cook garlic in hot oil over medium-high heat for 15 seconds. Add shrimp. Cook and stir for 2 to 3 minutes or until shrimp are opaque. Remove shrimp. In a small bowl, stir together broth, cornstarch, basil, and oregano. Add to skillet. Cook and stir until thickened and bubbly. Add the spinach. Cook for 1 to 2 minutes more or until wilted. Return shrimp to skillet; stir to combine.

3 Toss shrimp mixture and pasta together. Top with Parmesan cheese.

Nutrition facts per serving: 333 cal., 7 g total fat (1 g sat. fat), 136 mg chol., 422 mg sodium, 39 g carbo., 25 g pro.

saucy SHRIMP AND VEGGIES

Start to Finish: 20 minutes
Makes: 4 servings

1 12-ounce package peeled fresh baby carrots

8 ounces broccoli, trimmed and cut up (3 cups)

1 pound peeled and deveined medium shrimp

1 cup cherry tomatoes

1 tablespoon cooking oil

⅓ cup honey

2 tablespoons bottled chili-garlic sauce

2 tablespoons orange juice

1 In a large saucepan, cook carrots, covered, in lightly salted boiling water for 5 minutes. Add broccoli; cook for 3 to 4 minutes more or just until vegetables are tender. Drain.

2 Meanwhile, rinse shrimp; pat dry with paper towels. In a large skillet, cook and stir shrimp and tomatoes in hot oil for 3 to 4 minutes or until shrimp are opaque. Transfer to serving platter with vegetables. For sauce, in the skillet, combine honey, chili sauce, and orange juice; heat through. Spoon over shrimp and vegetables.

Nutrition facts per serving: 319 cal., 6 g total fat (1 g sat. fat), 172 mg chol., 361 mg sodium, 43 g carbo., 26 g pro.

citrus SCALLOPS

Start to Finish: 15 minutes
Makes: 4 servings

1 **pound fresh or frozen sea scallops**

1 **medium orange**

1 **tablespoon olive oil**

2 **cloves garlic, minced, or 1 teaspoon bottled minced garlic**

½ **teaspoon snipped fresh thyme**

Salt

Ground black pepper

1 Thaw scallops, if frozen. Rinse scallops; pat dry with paper towels. Set scallops aside. Finely shred 1 teaspoon peel from the orange. Cut orange in half; squeeze to get ⅓ cup juice.

2 In a large skillet, cook scallops in hot oil over medium-high heat for 2 to 3 minutes or until scallops are opaque, stirring frequently. Transfer scallops to a serving platter; keep warm.

3 For sauce, add garlic to skillet; cook and stir for 30 seconds (add more oil to skillet if necessary). Add orange peel, orange juice, and thyme to skillet. Bring to boiling; reduce heat. Simmer, uncovered, for 1 to 2 minutes or until desired consistency. Season with salt and pepper. Pour over scallops.

Nutrition facts per serving: 142 cal., 4 g total fat (1 g sat. fat), 37 mg chol., 218 mg sodium, 5 g carbo., 19 g pro.

salmon IN PARCHMENT

Start to Finish: 20 minutes
Oven: 375°F
Makes: 4 servings

4   skinless salmon fillets (about
    1¼ pounds total)

4   12-inch squares parchment
    paper

1   tablespoon olive oil or
    cooking oil

⅛   teaspoon ground black
    pepper

1   tablespoon snipped fresh
    mint

1   tablespoon snipped fresh dill
    or 1 teaspoon dried dillweed

4   thin slices lemon, quartered

1   tablespoon capers, drained

    Dill sprigs and/or lemon
    wedges (optional)

1 Preheat oven to 375°F. Rinse fish; pat dry with paper towels. Place one fish portion in the middle of each parchment square. Drizzle with olive oil and sprinkle with pepper. Top each with mint, dill, lemon pieces, and capers. Bring up two opposite sides of parchment and fold several times over fish. Fold remaining ends of parchment and tuck under. Place fish packets in a shallow baking pan.

2 Bake for 13 to 15 minutes or until fish flakes easily when tested with a fork, carefully opening one packet to test doneness. Carefully open each packet to serve. If desired, garnish with fresh dill sprigs and/or lemon wedges.

Nutrition facts per serving: 292 cal., 19 g total fat (4 g sat. fat), 84 mg chol., 148 mg sodium, 1 g carbo., 28 g pro.

tuna SALAD WITH CAPERS

Start to Finish: 20 minutes
Makes: 6 servings

½ cup mayonnaise or salad
   dressing
2 tablespoons capers, drained
2 tablespoons lemon juice
1 tablespoon snipped fresh
   tarragon
1 teaspoon Cajun seasoning or
   pepper blend
1 12-ounce can solid white
   tuna, drained
2 tablespoons milk
1 10-ounce package torn mixed
   greens (romaine blend) or
   8 cups torn romaine
2 cups packaged coleslaw mix
3 small tomatoes, cut into
   wedges

1 In a small bowl, combine mayonnaise, capers, lemon juice, tarragon, and Cajun seasoning. In a large bowl, flake tuna into large chunks; toss with 3 tablespoons of the mayonnaise mixture. Stir milk into remaining mayonnaise mixture. Divide greens among six plates; top with coleslaw mix, tuna, and tomato wedges. Serve with dressing.

Nutrition facts per serving: 228 cal., 17 g total fat (3 g sat. fat), 38 mg chol., 455 mg sodium, 5 g carbo., 15 g pro.

tuna-potato CAKES

Start to Finish: 18 minutes
Makes: 4 servings

1 cup packaged refrigerated mashed potatoes with garlic*

1 12-ounce can tuna (water pack), drained and broken into chunks

⅓ cup seasoned fine dry bread crumbs

½ cup finely chopped celery

¼ teaspoon ground black pepper

2 tablespoons cooking oil

1 In a medium bowl, combine potatoes, tuna, bread crumbs, celery, and pepper.

2 In a small skillet, heat oil over medium heat. Drop about ⅓ cup potato mixture into hot oil; flatten into a ½-inch patty. Cook for 4 minutes or until bottom is brown. Carefully turn; cook for 4 minutes more. Repeat with remaining mixture.

Nutrition facts per serving (2 cakes): 267 cal., 14 g total fat (2 g sat. fat), 22 mg chol., 621 mg sodium, 16 g carbo., 19 g pro.

*Test Kitchen Tip: Instead of packaged refrigerated mashed potatoes, use leftover mashed potatoes plus ¼ teaspoon garlic powder.

tilapia WITH GINGER-MARINATED CUCUMBERS

Start to Finish: 20 minutes
Makes: 4 servings

- ½ **cup cider vinegar**
- ¼ **cup packed brown sugar**
- 2 **teaspoons grated fresh ginger**
- ½ **teaspoon salt**
- 2 **medium cucumbers, sliced (about 3½ cups)**
- 2 **tablespoons coarsely chopped fresh mint**
- 4 **4-ounce tilapia fillets, ½ to ¾ inch thick**
- **Nonstick cooking spray**
- 1 **6-ounce carton plain yogurt**
- 1 **teaspoon packed brown sugar**
- **Lemon peel strips (optional)**
- **Cracked black pepper**

1 Preheat the broiler. In a medium bowl, stir together vinegar, ¼ cup brown sugar, ginger, and salt until sugar dissolves. Set aside ¼ cup of the mixture. Add cucumbers and half of the mint to remaining mixture; toss to coat and set aside.

2 Rinse fish; pat dry with paper towels. Lightly coat the rack of an unheated broiler pan with cooking spray; add tilapia. Brush the ¼ cup vinegar mixture over fish. Broil 4 inches from the heat for 4 to 6 minutes or until fish flakes easily when tested with a fork.

3 Meanwhile, in another small bowl, combine yogurt, remaining mint, and 1 teaspoon brown sugar.

4 Use a slotted spoon to place cucumbers on plates. Top with fish and yogurt mixture. Sprinkle with lemon peel strips, if desired, and cracked pepper.

Nutrition facts per serving: 210 cal., 3 g total fat (1 g sat. fat), 59 mg chol., 388 mg sodium, 23 g carbo., 26 g pro.

one-dish
MEALS

Pineapple-Chicken Stir-Fry, *recipe page 70*

mexican CHICKEN-TORTILLA SOUP

This soup features cilantro, a fresh herb that looks like a flattened parsley leaf but has a pungent, almost musty odor and taste that gives a distinctive flavor to Mexican dishes.

Prep: 25 minutes
Cook: 40 minutes
Makes: 4 servings

- 2 whole small chicken breasts (about 1¼ pounds total)
- 3½ cups chicken broth
- ½ cup chopped onion
- 1 clove garlic, minced
- ½ teaspoon ground cumin
- 1 tablespoon cooking oil
- 1 14.5-ounce can tomatoes, cut up
- 1 8-ounce can tomato sauce
- 1 4-ounce can whole green chile peppers, rinsed, seeded, and cut into thin, bite-size strips
- ¼ cup snipped cilantro or parsley
- 1 tablespoon snipped fresh oregano or 1 teaspoon dried oregano, crushed
- 6 6-inch corn tortillas
  Cooking oil
- 1 cup shredded cheddar or Monterey Jack cheese (4 ounces)

1 Rinse chicken. In a large saucepan or Dutch oven, combine chicken and chicken broth. Bring to boiling; reduce heat. Cover and simmer for about 15 minutes or until chicken is tender and no longer pink. Remove chicken. Set aside to cool. Skin, bone, and finely shred chicken. Set chicken aside. Discard skin and bones. Strain broth through a large sieve or colander lined with two layers of 100-percent-cotton cheesecloth. Skim fat from broth and set broth aside.

2 In the same saucepan, cook onion, garlic, and cumin in 1 tablespoon hot oil until onion is tender. Stir in strained broth, undrained tomatoes, tomato sauce, chile peppers, cilantro or parsley, and oregano. Bring to boiling; reduce heat. Cover and simmer for 20 minutes. Stir in shredded chicken. Heat through.

3 Meanwhile, cut tortillas in half, then cut crosswise into ½-inch-wide strips. In a heavy medium skillet, heat ¼ inch oil. Cook strips in hot oil, half at a time, for about 1 minute or until crisp and light brown. Remove with a slotted spoon; drain on paper towels.

4 Divide fried tortilla strips among soup bowls. Ladle soup over tortilla strips. Sprinkle each serving with shredded cheese. Serve immediately.

Nutrition facts per serving: 496 cal., 24 g total fat (8 g sat. fat), 85 mg chol., 1,658 mg sodium, 33 g carbo., 38 g pro.

white CHILI WITH SALSA VERDE

This wintertime dish looks like navy bean soup and tastes like a mild-flavored chili. Unlike ordinary chili, however, it's topped with a spicy Mexican salsa that's made with tomatillos.

Prep: 20 minutes
Cook: 30 minutes
Makes: 4 servings

12 **ounces ground turkey**

½ **cup chopped onion**

1 **clove garlic, minced**

3 **cups water**

1 **15-ounce can Great Northern or white kidney (cannellini) beans, rinsed and drained**

1 **4-ounce can diced green chile peppers**

2 **teaspoons instant chicken bouillon granules**

1 **teaspoon ground cumin**

¼ **teaspoon ground black pepper**

¼ **cup water**

2 **tablespoons all-purpose flour**

1 **cup shredded Monterey Jack cheese (4 ounces)**

Salsa Verde*

1 In a large saucepan or Dutch oven, cook ground turkey, onion, and garlic until turkey is brown. Drain off fat, if necessary. Stir in the 3 cups water, the beans, undrained chili peppers, chicken bouillon granules, cumin, and black pepper.

2 Bring to boiling; reduce heat. Cover and simmer for 30 minutes. Stir together the ¼ cup water and the flour; stir into bean mixture. Cook and stir until thickened and bubbly. Cook and stir for 1 minute more. Top each serving with cheese and Salsa Verde.

*Salsa Verde: In a medium bowl, stir together 5 or 6 fresh tomatillos (6 to 8 ounces), husks removed and finely chopped, or one 13-ounce can tomatillos, rinsed, drained, and finely chopped; 2 tablespoons finely chopped onion; 2 fresh serrano or jalapeño peppers, seeded and finely chopped; 1 tablespoon snipped fresh cilantro or parsley; 1 teaspoon finely shredded lime peel; and ½ teaspoon sugar. Cover and chill for up to 2 days or freeze; thaw before using.

Nutrition facts per serving: 319 cal., 16 g total fat (7 g sat. fat),57 mg chol., 927 mg sodium, 24 g carbo., 26 g pro.

thai-style VEGGIE PIZZA

Prep: 20 minutes
Bake: 5 minutes
Oven: 450°F
Makes: 2 servings

1 **8-inch Italian bread shell (such as Boboli)**

Nonstick cooking spray

½ **cup sliced fresh shiitake or button mushrooms**

⅓ **cup fresh pea pods, cut into thin strips**

2 **tablespoons coarsely shredded carrot**

2 **tablespoons sliced green onion**

2 **to 3 tablespoons bottled peanut sauce**

1 **tablespoon chopped peanuts**

Fresh cilantro leaves

1 Preheat oven to 450°F. Place bread shell on an ungreased baking sheet. Bake for 5 to 7 minutes or until light brown and crisp. Meanwhile, lightly coat an unheated medium nonstick skillet with nonstick cooking spray. Preheat skillet over medium heat. Add mushrooms, pea pods, and carrot; cook for about 2 minutes or just until tender. Stir in green onion. Remove from heat.

2 Carefully spread hot bread shell with peanut sauce. Top with hot vegetable mixture; sprinkle with peanuts and cilantro leaves. Cut in half to serve.

Nutrition facts per serving: 283 cal., 10 g total fat (3 g sat. fat), 0 mg chol., 634 mg sodium, 40 g carbo., 11 g pro.

scalloped POTATOES AND HAM

Prep: 15 minutes
Bake: 45 minutes
Stand: 10 minutes
Oven: 350°F
Makes: 6 to 8 servings

1 **10.75-ounce can condensed cream of onion or cream of celery soup**

½ **cup milk**

⅛ **teaspoon ground black pepper**

1 **pound cooked ham, cubed**

1 **20-ounce package refrigerated diced potatoes with onion**

¾ **cup shredded Swiss or cheddar cheese (3 ounces)**

① Preheat oven to 350°F. In a large bowl, stir together soup, milk, and pepper. Stir in ham and potatoes. Transfer to an ungreased 2-quart rectangular baking dish.

② Bake, covered, for 40 minutes. Stir mixture; sprinkle with cheese. Bake, uncovered, for 5 to 10 minutes more or until heated through and cheese melts. Let stand for 10 minutes before serving.

Nutrition facts per serving: 332 cal., 14 g total fat (6 g sat. fat), 64 mg chol., 1,613 mg sodium, 29 g carbo., 21 g pro.

ham AND CHEESE CALZONES

Prep: 15 minutes
Bake: 15 minutes
Stand: 5 minutes
Oven: 400°F
Makes: 4 servings

1 **13.8-ounce package refrigerated pizza dough (for 1 crust)**

¼ **cup coarse-grain mustard**

6 **ounces sliced Swiss or provolone cheese**

1½ **cups cubed cooked ham (8 ounces)**

½ **teaspoon caraway seeds**

1 Preheat oven to 400°F. Line a baking sheet with foil; lightly grease foil. Set aside.

2 Unroll pizza dough. On a lightly floured surface, roll or pat dough into a 15x10-inch rectangle. Cut dough in half crosswise and lengthwise to make four rectangles. Spread mustard over rectangles. Divide half of the cheese among rectangles, placing cheese on half of each rectangle and cutting or tearing to fit as necessary. Top with ham and sprinkle with caraway seeds. Top with remaining cheese. Brush edges with water. For each calzone, fold dough over filling to opposite edge, stretching slightly if necessary. Seal edges with the tines of a fork. Place calzones on prepared baking sheet. Prick tops to allow steam to escape.

3 Bake for about 15 minutes or until golden. Let stand for 5 minutes before serving.

Nutrition facts per serving: 421 cal., 21 g total fat (10 g sat. fat), 72 mg chol., 1,390 mg sodium, 28 g carbo., 30 g pro.

meatball LASAGNA

Prep: 25 minutes
Bake: 45 minutes
Stand: 15 minutes
Makes: 8 to 9 servings

9 dried lasagna noodles

½ of a 15-ounce container ricotta cheese

1½ cups shredded mozzarella cheese (6 ounces)

¼ cup grated Parmesan cheese

1 16-ounce package frozen cooked Italian-style meatballs (½-ounce size), thawed

1 16-ounce jar tomato pasta sauce

1 Preheat oven to 375°F. Cook lasagna noodles according to package directions. Drain noodles; rinse with cold water. Drain well; set aside.

2 In a small bowl, stir together ricotta, 1 cup mozzarella cheese, and the Parmesan cheese; set aside. In a medium bowl, stir together meatballs and one-third (about 1 cup) of the pasta sauce; set aside.

3 To assemble, spread a small amount of the reserved sauce over bottom of a 2-quart square baking dish. Layer three cooked noodles in the dish. Spoon meatball mixture over noodles. Layer three more noodles over meatballs. Spread half of the remaining sauce over noodles. Spoon ricotta mixture over sauce and spread evenly. Top with remaining noodles and remaining sauce.

4 Cover dish with foil. Bake for 35 minutes. Remove foil and sprinkle remaining mozzarella over lasagna. Bake, uncovered, for about 10 minutes more or until cheese melts. Let stand for 15 minutes before serving.

Nutrition facts per serving: 410 cal., 21 g total fat (11 g sat. fat), 66 mg chol., 897 mg sodium, 31 g carbo., 23 g pro.

mama's AMAZING ZITI

Prep: 20 minutes
Cook: 25 minutes
Makes: 6 servings

1 **pound lean ground beef**

2 **cups shredded carrots**

2 **10.75-ounce cans reduced-fat and reduced-sodium condensed tomato soup**

2½ **cups water**

8 **ounces dried ziti**

2 **tablespoons snipped fresh basil or 2 teaspoons dried basil, crushed**

1 **teaspoon onion powder**

1 **teaspoon garlic powder**

1 **cup shredded part-skim mozzarella cheese (4 ounces)**

¼ **cup shredded Parmesan cheese (1 ounce)**

1 In a 4-quart Dutch oven, cook ground beef and carrots over medium heat until meat is brown. Drain off fat. Stir tomato soup, the water, uncooked ziti, dried basil (if using), onion powder, and garlic powder into meat mixture.

2 Bring mixture to boiling; reduce heat. Cook, covered, for about 25 minutes or until ziti is tender, stirring occasionally. Stir in fresh basil (if using) and mozzarella cheese. Sprinkle individual servings with Parmesan cheese.

Nutrition facts per serving: 420 cal., 11 g total fat (4 g sat. fat), 73 mg chol., 649 mg sodium, 49 g carbo., 32 g pro.

zippy BEEF, MAC, AND CHEESE

Nothing goes better with this old favorite than a fresh side salad. Simply peel and section oranges and cut jicama into strips; arrange on a lettuce leaf and drizzle with an oil-and-vinegar dressing.

Start to Finish: 30 minutes
Makes: 4 servings

- 6 **ounces dried elbow macaroni or corkscrew pasta (about 1½ cups)**
- 12 **ounces lean ground beef, lean ground pork, or uncooked ground turkey**
- 1 **15-ounce can tomato sauce**
- 1 **14.5-ounce can stewed tomatoes or Mexican-style stewed tomatoes**
- 4 **ounces American or sharp American cheese, cut into small pieces**
- 1 **tablespoon chili powder**
  Finely shredded or grated Parmesan cheese

1 In a 3-quart saucepan, cook pasta according to package directions; drain. Meanwhile, in a large skillet, cook ground meat until brown. Drain off fat.

2 Stir ground meat, tomato sauce, undrained tomatoes, American cheese, and chili powder into cooked pasta. Cook and stir over medium heat for 6 to 8 minutes or until heated through. Sprinkle each serving with Parmesan cheese.

Nutrition facts per serving: 342 cal., 15 g total fat (7 g sat. fat), 55 mg chol., 957 mg sodium, 32 g carbo., 20 g pro.

pasta WITH SAUSAGE-TOMATO SAUCE

Start to Finish: 30 minutes
Makes: 4 servings

- 8 **ounces dried penne, fettuccine, linguine, or rotelle**
- 1 **pound sweet or hot Italian sausage links**
- 1½ **cups water**
- 2 **medium fennel bulbs, cut into thin wedges (about 2 cups)**
- 1 **26-ounce jar tomato pasta sauce**
- ⅓ **cup water**

1 Cook pasta according to package directions; drain.

2 Meanwhile, cut sausage into 1-inch pieces. In a large skillet, combine sausage and the 1½ cups water. Heat to boiling. Cook, uncovered, on high for 10 minutes; drain off fat and return sausage to skillet. Add fennel and cook for 3 to 4 minutes or until sausage is brown and fennel is crisp-tender. Add pasta sauce and the ⅓ cup water. Heat to boiling; reduce heat. Simmer, covered, for 5 minutes. Serve with the pasta.

Nutrition facts per serving: 714 cal., 38 g total fat (13 g sat. fat), 86 mg chol., 1,474 mg sodium, 65 g carbo., 28 g pro.

baked RATATOUILLE-SAUSAGE PENNE

Prep: 35 minutes
Bake: 35 minutes
Oven: 350°F
Makes: 6 servings

- **3 turkey Italian sausage links (12 ounces total)**
- **4 cloves garlic, minced**
- **1 teaspoon olive oil**
- **1 14.5-ounce can no-salt-added diced tomatoes, undrained**
- **3 tablespoons snipped fresh parsley**
- **¼ teaspoon crushed red pepper (optional)**
- **1 pound eggplant, peeled and cut into ½-inch cubes**
- **6 ounces dried whole wheat penne (about 2¼ cups)**
- **⅓ cup finely shredded Parmesan cheese**
- **Snipped fresh parsley (optional)**

1 Preheat oven to 350°F. Place sausage links in an unheated skillet with ½ inch of water. Bring to boiling; reduce heat. Simmer, covered, for about 15 minutes or until juices run clear; drain off liquid. Cook for 2 to 4 minutes more or until brown, turning occasionally. Remove from heat. When cool enough to handle, cut sausages in half lengthwise; bias-cut into ½-inch slices. Set aside.

2 In a large skillet, cook garlic in hot oil for 1 minute. Stir in undrained tomatoes, 3 tablespoons parsley, and, if desired, crushed red pepper. Bring to boiling. Stir in eggplant. Reduce heat. Simmer, covered, for 15 minutes.

3 Meanwhile, cook pasta according to package directions, cooking it for the minimum time listed; drain. Return pasta to hot pan. Stir in eggplant mixture and sausage. Spoon into a 2-quart baking dish.

4 Bake, covered, for about 30 minutes or until heated through. Sprinkle with Parmesan cheese. Uncover; bake for about 5 minutes more or until cheese melts. If desired, sprinkle with additional parsley.

Nutrition facts per serving: 251 cal., 8 g total fat (2 g sat. fat), 39 mg chol., 559 mg sodium, 30 g carbo., 17 g pro.

turkey TETRAZZINI

Tetrazzini is a quick supper when cooked in a wok—there's plenty of room for tossing the spaghetti with the turkey, mushrooms, and creamy sauce.

Start to Finish: 35 minutes
Makes: 4 servings

12 ounces turkey breast
tenderloin

1⅔ cups milk

2 tablespoons all-purpose flour

2 teaspoons instant chicken
bouillon granules

⅛ teaspoon ground black pepper

¼ cup slivered almonds

1 tablespoon cooking oil

1 cup sliced fresh mushrooms

2 green onions, sliced (¼ cup)

2 tablespoons dry white wine,
dry sherry, or milk

4 ounces dried thin spaghetti,
cooked and drained

¼ cup finely shredded Parmesan
cheese

2 tablespoons snipped fresh
parsley

Tomato slices (optional)

Fresh parsley sprigs (optional)

1 Cut turkey into thin, bite-size strips. For sauce, in a small bowl stir together milk, flour, chicken bouillon granules, and pepper. Set aside.

2 Preheat a wok or large skillet over medium-high heat. Stir-fry almonds in hot wok for 2 to 3 minutes or until golden brown. Remove almonds from wok. Let wok cool slightly.

3 Add oil to cooled wok. Preheat over medium-high heat (add more oil if necessary during cooking). Stir-fry mushrooms and green onions in hot oil for 1 to 2 minutes or until tender. Remove the mushroom mixture from wok.

4 Add turkey to wok. Stir-fry for 2 to 3 minutes or until no longer pink. Push turkey from center of wok. Stir sauce; add to center of wok. Cook and stir until thickened and bubbly. Cook and stir for 2 minutes more.

5 Stir in wine, sherry, or milk. Return cooked mushroom mixture to wok. Add cooked spaghetti, Parmesan cheese, and the snipped parsley. Toss all ingredients together to coat. Cook and stir for 1 to 2 minutes more or until heated through. Sprinkle with toasted almonds. Serve immediately. If desired, garnish with tomato and parsley sprigs.

Nutrition facts per serving: 376 cal., 13 g total fat (4 g sat. fat), 50 mg chol., 637 mg sodium, 34 g carbo., 28 g pro.

mediterranean PIZZA SKILLET

Prep: 20 minutes
Cook: 10 minutes
Makes: 4 servings

3 medium skinless, boneless chicken breast halves, cut into ¾-inch pieces

2 cloves garlic, minced

2 tablespoons olive oil

4 roma tomatoes, chopped

1 14-ounce can artichoke hearts, drained and quartered

1 2.25-ounce can sliced pitted ripe olives, drained

½ teaspoon dried Italian seasoning, crushed

¼ teaspoon ground black pepper

2 cups romaine, chopped (2 ounces)

1 cup crumbled feta cheese (4 ounces)

⅓ cup fresh basil leaves, shredded or torn

Crusty Italian or French bread, sliced

1 In a large skillet, cook and stir chicken and garlic in hot oil over medium-high heat until chicken is brown. Stir in tomatoes, artichokes, olives, seasoning, and pepper. Bring to boiling; reduce heat. Simmer, covered, for 10 minutes or until chicken is no longer pink. Top with lettuce and cheese. Cook, covered, for 1 to 2 minutes more or until lettuce starts to wilt. Sprinkle with basil and serve on or with bread.

Nutrition facts per serving: 395 cal., 17 g total fat (6 g sat. fat), 82 mg chol., 1,003 mg sodium, 27 g carbo., 33 g pro.

chicken THIGHS AND ORZO

Prep: 20 minutes
Cook: 25 minutes
Makes: 6 servings

1 **4-ounce package pancetta, chopped, or 4 slices bacon, chopped**

Olive oil

6 **chicken thighs (about 2¼ pounds), skinned**

2 **14.5-ounce cans diced tomatoes with garlic and onion, undrained**

1 **cup dried orzo**

2 **cloves garlic, minced**

1 **cup water**

⅓ **cup pitted kalamata olives**

¼ **cup snipped fresh basil**

1 **6-ounce bag prewashed baby spinach leaves**

3 **ounces goat cheese with basil and roasted garlic (about ⅓ cup)**

1 In a 5- to 6-quart Dutch oven, cook pancetta until brown. Remove pancetta, reserving 2 tablespoons drippings in pan (add olive oil if necessary to equal 2 tablespoons). Drain pancetta on paper towels; set aside. Cook chicken in drippings for about 10 minutes or until light brown, turning to brown evenly; drain off fat. Add undrained tomatoes, orzo, garlic, and the water. Bring to boiling; reduce heat.

2 Simmer, covered, for 25 to 30 minutes or until chicken is no longer pink (180°F) and orzo is tender. If necessary, cook, uncovered, for 2 to 3 minutes or until sauce is desired consistency. Stir in pancetta, olives, and basil; heat through. Divide spinach among six plates. Top each with a thigh, some of the orzo mixture, and some of the cheese.

Nutrition facts per serving: 395 cal., 18 g total fat (5 g sat. fat), 77 mg chol., 1,229 mg sodium, 32 g carbo., 26 g pro.

three-cheese LASAGNA

Prep: 50 minutes
Bake: 35 minutes
Stand: 15 minutes
Chill: up to 24 hours
Makes: 12 servings

2 medium eggplants, chopped (11 cups)
2 large red onions, halved crosswise and thickly sliced (about 2 cups)
2 cloves garlic, minced
1 cup snipped fresh basil
¼ cup olive oil
12 dried lasagna noodles
2 cups shredded Gruyère cheese (8 ounces)
1 15-ounce carton ricotta cheese
12 ounces goat cheese (chèvre)
1 cup whipping cream
2 eggs
½ teaspoon salt
½ teaspoon ground black pepper
¼ teaspoon crushed red pepper
2 teaspoons finely shredded lemon peel

1 Preheat oven to 450°F. In a roasting pan, combine eggplant, onion, and garlic. Add ½ cup of the basil and the oil; toss to coat. Roast, uncovered, for 30 to 35 minutes or until vegetables are very tender, stirring once.

2 Meanwhile, cook lasagna noodles according to package directions; drain. Set aside. For filling, in a food processor, combine 1½ cups of the Gruyère cheese, the ricotta, goat cheese, cream, eggs, salt, black pepper, and crushed red pepper. Process until just combined.

3 Reduce oven temperature to 375°F. Spoon one-third of the eggplant mixture evenly in the bottom of a 3-quart rectangular baking dish. Layer with 4 noodles and one-third of the filling. Repeat layers twice, starting with eggplant and ending with filling. Sprinkle with remaining ½ cup Gruyère cheese. Cover with lightly greased foil. Bake for 20 minutes. Uncover and bake for 15 to 20 minutes more or until heated through. Let stand for 15 minutes before serving. Sprinkle top with remaining ½ cup basil and the lemon peel.

Nutrition facts per serving: 439 cal., 30 g total fat (16 g sat. fat), 114 mg chol., 315 mg sodium, 23 g carbo., 20 g pro.

To Make Ahead: Cover unbaked lasagna with lightly greased foil and refrigerate for up to 24 hours. Bake, covered, in a 375°F oven for 40 minutes. Uncover and bake for 20 to 25 minutes more or until heated through. Let stand for 15 minutes before serving. Top as directed.

pasta WITH GREEN BEANS AND GOAT CHEESE

Prep: 15 minutes
Cook: 13 minutes
Makes: 6 servings

- 12 cups water
- ½ teaspoon salt
- 8 ounces dried linguine
- 1 9-ounce package frozen cut green beans
- 2 medium leeks, thinly sliced (about ⅔ cup)
- ½ cup chopped walnuts
- 2 tablespoons olive oil
- 1 tablespoon butter
- 1 tablespoon snipped fresh thyme or marjoram
- 4 ounces semisoft goat cheese (chèvre), crumbled

  Cracked black pepper

1 In a 4-quart Dutch oven, bring water and salt to boiling. Add linguine; boil for 5 minutes. Add green beans. Continue boiling for about 5 minutes more or until linguine is tender but still firm; drain well.

2 In the same Dutch oven, cook leeks and walnuts in hot olive oil and butter over medium heat for 3 to 4 minutes or until leeks are tender and walnuts are lightly toasted. Stir in thyme. Stir in drained linguine and green beans; heat through.

3 Transfer pasta mixture to a serving platter. Sprinkle with goat cheese and pepper. Serve immediately.

Nutrition facts per serving: 361 cal., 19 g total fat (6 g sat. fat), 20 mg chol., 219 mg sodium, 36 g carbo., 11 g pro.

campanelle WITH PEAS AND ARTICHOKES

Start to Finish: 20 minutes
Makes: 4 servings

8 ounces dried campanelle, radiatore, or rotini

1 cup frozen peas

½ cup frozen or canned artichoke hearts (rinse, if canned), coarsely chopped

2 cloves garlic, minced

½ cup chopped fresh tomato

½ cup finely shredded Pecorino Romano or Parmesan cheese

1 tablespoon extra-virgin olive oil

2 tablespoons lemon juice

⅛ teaspoon ground black pepper

¼ cup cooked ham, cut into slivers

Finely shredded Pecorino Romano or Parmesan cheese (optional)

1 Cook pasta according to package directions, adding frozen peas, frozen artichoke hearts (if using), and minced garlic for the last 3 minutes of cooking time. Drain, reserving ¼ cup of the pasta water.

2 In a large serving bowl, toss together drained pasta mixture, the pasta water, canned artichoke hearts (if using), tomato, ½ cup Pecorino Romano cheese, olive oil, lemon juice, and pepper. Toss to combine. Sprinkle with ham and, if desired, additional shredded cheese.

Nutrition facts per serving: 341 cal., 9 g total fat (3 g sat. fat), 18 mg chol., 314 mg sodium, 50 g carbo., 15 g pro.

ham AND CHEESE LASAGNA

Prep: 1 hour
Bake: 50 minutes
Stand: 20 minutes
Oven: 350°F
Makes: 12 servings

1 large onion, chopped (1 cup)

4 stalks celery, thinly sliced
(2 cups)

4 carrots, chopped (2 cups)

2 cloves garlic, minced

2 tablespoons olive oil

3 cups sliced cremini
mushrooms or other
small brown mushrooms
(8 ounces)

2 cups cubed cooked ham

2 cups whipping cream

1 14.5-ounce can diced
tomatoes with basil, garlic,
and oregano, undrained

½ cup water

¼ cup dry red wine

Salt

Ground black pepper

1 cup grated Parmesan cheese

1½ cups shredded Swiss cheese
(6 ounces)

12 no-boil lasagna noodles
(7 to 8 ounces)

1️⃣ Preheat oven to 350°F. For sauce, in a 12-inch skillet or Dutch oven, cook and stir onion, celery, carrots, and garlic in hot oil over medium heat for 10 minutes or until vegetables are just tender. Add mushrooms and ham. Cook, uncovered, for 10 minutes, stirring occasionally. Stir in cream, undrained tomatoes, the water, and wine. Bring to boiling; reduce heat. Simmer, uncovered, for 5 minutes. Season with salt and pepper.

2️⃣ Combine Parmesan and Swiss cheese. Spoon 1½ cups of the sauce into a 3-quart rectangular baking dish. Sprinkle with ⅔ cup of the cheese. Top with four lasagna noodles, overlapping as needed. Repeat layering twice. Spoon on remaining sauce and sprinkle with remaining cheese mixture. Cover tightly with foil. Bake for about 50 minutes or until heated through and noodles are tender. Let stand, covered, for 20 minutes before serving.

Nutrition facts per serving: 376 cal., 25 g total fat (14 g sat. fat), 86 mg chol., 671 mg sodium, 22 g carbo., 15 g pro.

horseradish-dill BEEF STROGANOFF

Follow this quick-prep method to make a classic Old World recipe. The horseradish–sour cream sauce is an imperial touch.

Start to Finish: 30 minutes
Makes: 4 servings

- 3 **cups dried wide noodles**
- 3 **cups broccoli florets (12 ounces)**
- ½ **cup light dairy sour cream**
- 1½ **teaspoons prepared horseradish**
- ½ **teaspoon snipped fresh dill**
- 1 **pound beef ribeye steak**
- 1 **small onion, cut into ½-inch slices**
- 1 **clove garlic, minced**
- 1 **tablespoon cooking oil**
- 4 **teaspoons all-purpose flour**
- ½ **teaspoon ground black pepper**
- 1 **14-ounce can beef broth**
- 3 **tablespoons tomato paste**
- 1 **teaspoon Worcestershire sauce**

1 Cook noodles according to package directions, adding broccoli for the last 5 minutes of cooking; drain. Cover and keep warm.

2 Meanwhile, for sauce, in a small bowl stir together the sour cream, horseradish, and dill. Cover and chill until serving time.

3 Trim fat from meat. Slice meat across the grain into bite-size strips. In a large skillet, cook half of the meat, the onion, and garlic in hot oil over medium-high heat for about 3 minutes or until meat is slightly pink in center. Remove from skillet. Repeat with the remaining meat. Return all meat mixture to skillet.

4 Sprinkle meat with flour and pepper; stir to coat. Stir in the beef broth, tomato paste, and Worcestershire sauce. Cook and stir until thickened and bubbly. Cook and stir for 1 minute more.

5 To serve, divide noodle mixture among bowls or dinner plates. Spoon meat mixture on top of noodle mixture. Spoon sauce on top of meat mixture.

Nutrition facts per serving: 368 cal., 15 g total fat (5 g sat. fat), 81 mg chol., 454 mg sodium, 32 g carbo., 29 g pro.

ginger BEEF STIR-FRY

Start to Finish: 25 minutes
Makes: 4 servings

8 ounces beef top round steak

½ cup reduced-sodium beef broth

3 tablespoons reduced-sodium soy sauce

2½ teaspoons cornstarch

2 to 3 teaspoons grated fresh ginger

Nonstick cooking spray

1½ cups sliced fresh mushrooms

1 medium carrot, thinly bias-sliced

3 cups small broccoli florets or 1 pound fresh asparagus spears, trimmed and cut into 2-inch pieces

1 small red sweet pepper, seeded and cut into thin strips (1 cup)

1 tablespoon cooking oil

2 green onions, bias-sliced into 2-inch pieces

2 cups hot cooked brown rice

1 If desired, partially freeze beef for easier slicing. Trim fat from beef. Thinly slice beef across the grain into bite-size strips. Set aside. For sauce, in a small bowl, stir together beef broth, soy sauce, cornstarch, and ginger; set aside.

2 Lightly coat an unheated wok or large nonstick skillet with cooking spray. Preheat over medium-high heat. Add mushrooms and carrot; stir-fry for 2 minutes. Add broccoli and sweet pepper; stir-fry for about 2 minutes more or until vegetables are crisp-tender. Remove from wok.

3 Carefully add oil to hot wok. Add beef; stir-fry for 2 to 3 minutes or to desired doneness. Push beef from center of wok. Stir sauce and add to center of wok. Cook and stir until thickened and bubbly.

4 Return vegetables to wok. Add green onions. Stir all ingredients to coat with sauce; heat through. Serve over brown rice.

Nutrition facts per serving: 274 cal., 7 g total fat (1 g sat. fat), 32 mg chol., 552 mg sodium, 34 g carbo., 20 g pro.

sesame ORANGE BEEF

Start to Finish: 25 minutes
Makes: 4 servings

8 ounces fresh green beans, halved crosswise

2 teaspoons sesame seeds

½ cup orange juice

2 tablespoons reduced-sodium soy sauce

1 tablespoon toasted sesame oil

1 teaspoon cornstarch

½ teaspoon finely shredded orange peel

Nonstick cooking spray

½ cup bias-sliced green onions

1 tablespoon grated fresh ginger

2 cloves garlic, minced

1 teaspoon cooking oil

12 ounces boneless beef sirloin steak, thinly sliced

2 cups hot cooked brown rice

2 oranges, peeled and thinly sliced crosswise

1 In a medium saucepan, cook green beans, covered, in a small amount of boiling water for 6 to 8 minutes or until crisp-tender. Drain; set aside.

2 Meanwhile, in a small skillet, cook sesame seeds over medium heat for 1 to 2 minutes or until toasted, watching closely and stirring frequently. Set aside.

3 For sauce, in a small bowl, combine orange juice, soy sauce, sesame oil, cornstarch, and orange peel; set aside.

4 Coat an unheated large nonstick skillet with cooking spray. Heat over medium-high heat. Add green onions, ginger, and garlic; cook and stir for 1 minute. Add green beans; cook and stir for 2 minutes. Remove vegetables from skillet.

5 Carefully add oil to hot skillet. Add beef; cook and stir for about 3 minutes or to desired doneness. Remove beef from skillet.

6 Stir sauce; add to skillet. Cook and stir until thickened and bubbly; cook and stir for 2 minutes more. Return meat and vegetables to skillet. Heat through, stirring to coat all ingredients with sauce. Serve over brown rice. Top with orange sections and sprinkle with toasted sesame seeds.

Nutrition facts per serving: 348 cal., 10 g total fat (2 g sat. fat), 52 mg chol., 341 mg sodium, 41 g carbo., 24 g pro.

pineapple-chicken
STIR-FRY

Start to Finish: 25 minutes
Makes: 4 servings

- 4 teaspoons cooking oil
- 1 medium red onion, halved lengthwise and sliced
- ¼ of a fresh pineapple, peeled, cored, and cut into bite-size pieces
- ¾ cup thin, bite-size strips zucchini
- ¾ cup trimmed fresh pea pods
- 12 ounces skinless, boneless chicken breast halves, cut into thin, bite-size strips
- 3 tablespoons bottled stir-fry sauce

1 In a wok or large skillet, heat 2 teaspoons of the oil over medium-high heat. Stir-fry red onion in hot oil for 2 minutes. Add pineapple, zucchini, and pea pods. Stir-fry for 2 minutes more. Remove mixture from wok.

2 Add the remaining 2 teaspoons oil to hot wok. Add chicken. Stir-fry for 2 to 3 minutes or until chicken is no longer pink. Return onion mixture to wok. Add stir-fry sauce. Cook and stir for about 1 minute or until heated through.

Nutrition facts per serving: 181 cal., 6 g total fat (1 g sat. fat), 49 mg chol., 440 mg sodium, 11 g carbo., 21 g pro.

thai PORK STIR-FRY

Prep: 35 minutes
Cook: 9 minutes
Makes: 6 servings

2 tablespoons olive oil
1 tablespoon reduced-sodium
   soy sauce
½ teaspoon garlic powder
½ teaspoon finely chopped
   fresh ginger or ¼ teaspoon
   ground ginger
½ teaspoon ground black
   pepper
½ teaspoon ground cardamom
½ teaspoon chili powder
1½ pounds boneless pork loin,
   cut into bite-size strips
2 cups broccoli florets
1 cup thinly sliced carrots
1 cup cauliflower florets
2 tablespoons white vinegar
1 tablespoon curry powder
2 cups hot cooked brown rice

1 In a very large skillet, combine oil, soy sauce, garlic powder, ginger, pepper, cardamom, and chili powder. Add half of the pork; cook and stir over medium-high heat for 3 minutes. Using a slotted spoon, remove pork from skillet. Repeat with the remaining pork. Return all of the pork to the skillet.

2 Add broccoli, carrots, cauliflower, vinegar, and curry powder to pork mixture. Bring to boiling; reduce heat. Simmer, covered, for 3 to 5 minutes or until vegetables are crisp-tender, stirring occasionally.

3 Serve pork and vegetables over brown rice.

Nutrition facts per serving: 301 cal., 11 g total fat (3 g sat. fat), 71 mg chol., 206 mg sodium, 21 g carbo., 28 g pro.

shredded PORK ROAST AND TOMATO TACOS

Prep: 10 minutes
Cook: 5 minutes
Makes: 8 servings

- 1 **17-ounce package refrigerated cooked pork roast**
- 1 **10-ounce can diced tomatoes and green chiles, undrained**
- 2 **teaspoons taco seasoning**
- 8 **taco shells**
- ½ **cup shredded lettuce**
- ½ **cup shredded cheddar cheese (2 ounces)**
  Dairy sour cream
  Purchased salsa

1 In a large skillet, combine pork, undrained tomatoes, and taco seasoning; bring to boiling. Reduce heat; boil gently, uncovered, for 5 minutes. Remove from heat. Using two forks, carefully shred pork.

2 To serve, remove meat and tomatoes from skillet with a slotted spoon. Spoon meat mixture into taco shells. Top with shredded lettuce and cheddar cheese. Serve with sour cream and salsa.

Nutrition facts per serving: 206 cal., 11 g total fat (5 g sat. fat), 49 mg chol., 529 mg sodium, 12 g carbo., 16 g pro.

super
SUPPERS

Chicken and Mushrooms, *recipe page 98*

pan-seared LAMB CHOPS WITH FRESH MINT SALAD

For the best color and flavor, let the lamb chops cook in the skillet, moving them only once to flip them.

Start to Finish: 30 minutes
Makes: 4 servings

¼ cup snipped fresh mint

¼ cup snipped fresh parsley

¼ cup crumbled feta cheese (1 ounce)

¼ cup chopped pecans, toasted

8 lamb rib chops or loin chops, cut 1 inch thick (about 2 pounds total)

2 teaspoons olive oil

¼ teaspoon salt

⅛ teaspoon ground black pepper

Olive oil (optional)

Lemon juice (optional)

Salad greens (optional)

1 In a small bowl, combine mint, parsley, feta cheese, and pecans; set aside.

2 Trim fat from chops. Rub chops with the 2 teaspoons olive oil; sprinkle with the salt and pepper. Preheat a large heavy skillet over medium-high heat until very hot. Add chops. Cook for 8 to 10 minutes or until well browned and medium doneness (145°F), turning chops once halfway through cooking.

3 To serve, sprinkle chops with mint mixture. If desired, drizzle additional olive oil and/or lemon juice over mint mixture and serve with salad greens.

Nutrition facts per serving: 252 cal., 17 g total fat (5 g sat. fat), 72 mg chol., 311 mg sodium, 2 g carbo., 22 g pro.

lamb CHOPS WITH TOMATOES

An aromatic balsamic-flavored tomato sauce brings out the best in succulent grilled lamb chops.

Start to Finish: 20 minutes
Makes: 4 servings

8 lamb loin chops, cut 1 inch thick

Salt

Ground black pepper

1 8.8-ounce pouch cooked long grain rice

4 medium roma tomatoes, cut up

4 green onions, cut into 1-inch pieces

1 tablespoon snipped fresh oregano

1 tablespoon balsamic vinegar

1 Season chops with salt and pepper. Place chops on the rack of an uncovered grill directly over medium coals. Grill for 12 to 14 minutes for medium-rare (145°F), turning once halfway through grilling.

2 Meanwhile, microwave rice according to package directions. In food processor, combine tomatoes, green onions, and oregano; process with on/off turns until coarsely chopped. Transfer to bowl; stir in vinegar. Season with salt and pepper. Arrange chops on rice and top with tomato mixture.

Nutrition facts per serving: 273 cal., 7 g total fat (2 g sat. fat), 70 mg chol., 153 mg sodium, 26 g carbo., 25 g pro.

cheese-topped STEAKS

Prep: 20 minutes
Grill: 15 minutes
Makes: 4 servings

2 ounces Gorgonzola cheese or other blue cheese, crumbled (½ cup)

¼ cup cooked bacon pieces

¼ cup pine nuts or slivered almonds, toasted

2 tablespoons fresh thyme leaves

2 cloves garlic, minced

¼ teaspoon ground black pepper

4 boneless beef top loin steaks, cut 1 inch thick

1 In a small bowl, combine cheese, bacon, nuts, thyme, garlic, and pepper; set aside.

2 Sprinkle steaks lightly with salt. For a charcoal grill, grill steaks on rack of an uncovered grill directly over medium heat to desired doneness, turning once halfway through grilling. Allow 10 to 12 minutes for medium-rare (145°F) or 12 to 15 minutes for medium (160°F). (For a gas grill, preheat grill. Reduce heat to medium. Place steaks on grill rack over heat. Cover and grill as above.)

3 To serve, top steaks with cheese mixture. Grill for 1 to 2 minutes or until cheese is soft.

Nutrition facts per serving: 640 cal., 30 g total fat (11 g sat. fat), 181 mg chol., 616 mg sodium, 3 g carbo., 86 g pro.

southwest PORK CHOPS

Start to Finish: 30 minutes
Makes: 6 servings

6 pork rib chops, cut ¾ inch
   thick
   Nonstick cooking spray
1 **15-ounce can Mexican- or
   Tex-Mex-style chili beans**
1 **cup bottled salsa**
1 **cup frozen whole kernel corn**
3 **cups hot cooked rice**
   **Snipped fresh cilantro
   (optional)**

1 Trim fat from chops. Coat a 12-inch nonstick skillet with nonstick cooking spray. Heat skillet over medium-high heat. Add chops, half at a time if necessary, to skillet; cook for about 2 minutes per side or until brown. Remove chops from skillet.

2 Add chili beans, salsa, and corn to skillet; stir to combine. Place chops on top of bean mixture. Bring to boiling; reduce heat. Simmer, covered, for 15 to 20 minutes or until chops are done (160°F). Serve over hot cooked rice. If desired, sprinkle with cilantro.

Nutrition facts per serving: 379 cal., 10 g total fat (3 g sat. fat), 71 mg chol., 490 mg sodium, 38 g carbo., 33 g pro.

memphis-style PORK CHOPS

Stop by your favorite deli or supermarket to pick up coleslaw or potato salad to go along with these fork-tender chops.

Prep: 15 minutes
Grill: 12 minutes
Makes: 4 servings

½ cup bottled chili sauce

2 tablespoons molasses

2 tablespoons cider vinegar

1 teaspoon chili powder

4 boneless pork loin chops,
   cut ¾ to 1 inch thick (about
   1¼ pounds total)

1 teaspoon dried basil, crushed

½ teaspoon paprika

¼ teaspoon salt

¼ teaspoon onion powder

¼ teaspoon cayenne pepper

1 In a small saucepan, stir together chili sauce, molasses, vinegar, and chili powder. Bring to boiling; reduce heat. Simmer, uncovered, for 3 minutes. Remove from heat.

2 Trim fat from chops. In a small bowl, stir together basil, paprika, salt, onion powder, and cayenne pepper. Sprinkle evenly over both sides of each chop; rub in with your fingers.

3 Place chops on the rack of an uncovered grill directly over medium coals. Grill for 12 to 15 minutes or until juices run clear (160°F), turning once and brushing with chili sauce mixture during the last 5 minutes of grilling.

Nutrition facts per serving: 260 cal., 7 g total fat (3 g sat. fat), 83 mg chol., 623 mg sodium, 16 g carbo., 31 g pro

pork SCALOPPINE WITH MUSTARD AND ROSEMARY

To keep the pork warm while you prepare the mushroom mixture, place the cooked pork slices on a warm serving platter. Cover with foil and place the platter in a 300°F oven.

Start to Finish: 35 minutes
Makes: 4 servings

- 1 **pound pork tenderloin**
- ⅓ **cup all-purpose flour**
- ½ **teaspoon ground black pepper**
- ¼ **teaspoon salt**
- 2 **teaspoons margarine or butter**
- 1 **tablespoon olive oil or cooking oil**
- 1 **cup sliced fresh mushrooms**
- 1 **tablespoon snipped fresh rosemary or 1 teaspoon dried rosemary, crushed**
- 2 **cloves garlic, minced**
- ¾ **cup chicken broth**
- 2 **tablespoons Dijon-style mustard**
- 1 **teaspoon finely shredded lemon peel**
- 1 **tablespoon lemon juice**
  Lemon wedges (optional)
  Fresh rosemary sprigs (optional)

1 Trim any fat from meat. Cut meat crosswise into ½-inch slices. Place each slice between two pieces of plastic wrap. With the heel of your hand, press each slice until about ⅛ inch thick. Remove plastic wrap.

2 In a shallow dish, combine flour, pepper, and salt. Coat meat with flour mixture, shaking off excess.

3 In a large skillet, heat margarine or butter and oil over medium-high heat. Add half of the meat; cook for 3 to 4 minutes or until slightly pink in center, turning once. Remove from skillet, reserving drippings in skillet. Cover and keep warm. Repeat with the remaining meat.

4 Reduce heat to medium. Add mushrooms, snipped fresh or dried rosemary, and garlic to reserved drippings in skillet. Cook and stir just until mushrooms are tender. Add broth, scraping up any browned bits on bottom. Bring to boiling. Boil gently, uncovered, for about 5 minutes or until reduced by half. Stir in Dijon mustard, lemon peel, and lemon juice. Heat through.

5 Serve the mushroom mixture over meat. If desired, garnish with lemon wedges and fresh rosemary sprigs.

Nutrition facts per serving: 287 cal., 14 g total fat (3 g sat. fat), 81 mg chol., 594 mg sodium, 10 g carbo., 28 g pro.

blue CHEESE 'N' CHOPS

Looking for something impressive to serve guests? Try these herb-rubbed pork chops. Pan-sizzled in their own juices, the chops are then baked along with rice. Fresh pear and blue cheese are the final touch.

Prep: 15 minutes
Bake: 30 minutes
Makes: 4 servings

Nonstick cooking spray

2½ **cups cooked brown rice**

 4 **green onions, sliced (½ cup)**

⅓ **cup apple juice**

¼ **cup chopped toasted walnuts (optional)**

¼ **teaspoon salt**

⅛ **teaspoon ground black pepper**

 1 **teaspoon dried thyme, crushed**

¼ **teaspoon salt**

¼ **to ½ teaspoon ground black pepper**

 4 **boneless pork loin chops, cut ½ to ¾ inch thick (about 12 ounces total)**

 1 **red pear, cored and chopped**

¼ **cup crumbled blue cheese**

1 Preheat oven to 350°F. Spray a 2-quart square baking dish and a large skillet with nonstick cooking spray; set aside. In a large bowl, combine the cooked rice, green onions, 2 tablespoons of the apple juice, the walnuts (if desired), ¼ teaspoon salt, and the ⅛ teaspoon pepper. Spoon rice mixture into prepared baking dish.

2 In a small bowl, stir together the thyme, ¼ teaspoon salt, and the ¼ to ½ teaspoon pepper. Rub onto both sides of chops. Cook chops in skillet over medium-high heat until browned, turning once. Arrange browned chops on top of rice mixture. Pour remaining apple juice over chops.

3 Bake, covered, for about 30 minutes or until no pink remains in chops and juices run clear. Transfer chops to serving plates. Stir chopped pear and blue cheese into hot rice mixture; serve with chops.

Nutrition facts per serving: 305 cal., 9 g total fat (5 g sat. fat), 45 mg chol., 416 mg sodium, 38 g carbo., 17 g pro.

szechwan PORK WITH PEPPERS

Green and red sweet peppers and the spicy sweetness of hoisin sauce contrast nicely with the pleasant heat of this dish. But if you prefer more heat than sweet, simply add more hot bean sauce.

Prep: 10 minutes
Cook: 10 minutes
Freeze: 30 minutes
Makes: 4 servings

- **12 ounces lean boneless pork**
- **3 tablespoons bottled hoisin sauce**
- **1 tablespoon hot bean sauce or hot bean paste**
- **1 tablespoon soy sauce**
- **1 teaspoon sugar**
- **1 tablespoon cooking oil**
- **4 cloves garlic, thinly sliced**
- **1 teaspoon grated fresh ginger**
- **2 medium red sweet peppers, cut into 1-inch pieces (2 cups)**
- **2 medium green sweet peppers, cut into 1-inch pieces (2 cups)**
- **2 cups hot cooked noodles or rice**

① Trim fat from meat. Partially freeze meat. Thinly slice across the grain into bite-size strips. Set aside. For sauce, in a small bowl stir together hoisin sauce, bean sauce or paste, soy sauce, and sugar. Set aside.

② Add oil to a wok or large skillet. Preheat over medium-high heat (add more oil if necessary during cooking). Stir-fry garlic and ginger in hot oil for 15 seconds. Add sweet peppers; stir-fry for 3 to 4 minutes or until crisp-tender. Remove pepper mixture from wok.

③ Add meat to wok. Stir-fry for 2 to 3 minutes or until meat is slightly pink in center. Push meat from center of wok. Add sauce to center of wok. Cook and stir until bubbly.

④ Return pepper mixture to wok. Stir all ingredients together to coat. Cook and stir for about 1 minute more or until heated through. Serve immediately over hot cooked noodles or rice.

Nutrition facts per serving: 292 cal., 10 g total fat (3 g sat. fat), 63 mg chol., 1,324 mg sodium, 32 g carbo., 18 g pro.

Great-Tasting Ginger

Many stir-fries depend on spicy-sweet ginger for its tempting flavor. Look for this knobby root in your supermarket's produce section. Grate or slice as much as you need (peeling isn't necessary). Wrap the remaining root in paper towels and refrigerate it for up to 1 week. Or cut up the ginger and place it in a small jar. Fill the jar with dry sherry or wine and refrigerate it, covered, for up to 3 months.

mustard-orange PORK TENDERLOIN

A mixture of vegetables, such as cut-up red onions, baby carrots, and chunks of zucchini, can be roasted alongside the meat. Just spray the vegetables with olive oil–flavored nonstick cooking spray before placing them in the pan around the meat.

Prep: 15 minutes
Roast: 25 minutes
Stand: 10 minutes
Makes: 4 servings

12 **ounces pork tenderloin**

½ **cup apricot preserves or orange marmalade**

3 **tablespoons Dijon-style mustard**

Nonstick cooking spray

2 **cups sliced fresh mushrooms**

½ **cup sliced green onions**

2 **tablespoons orange juice**

1 Preheat oven to 425°F. Trim fat from meat. Place meat on a rack in a shallow roasting pan. Insert a meat thermometer into the center of meat. Roast, uncovered, for 10 minutes.

2 Meanwhile, in a small bowl stir together preserves or marmalade and mustard. Spoon half of the mustard mixture over the meat. Set the remaining mustard mixture aside.

3 Roast for 15 to 25 minutes more or until the meat thermometer registers 155°F. Transfer the meat to a warm platter and cover with foil. Let stand for 10 minutes before slicing. (The meat's temperature will rise 5° during standing.)

4 Meanwhile, spray a medium saucepan with nonstick cooking spray. Add mushrooms and green onions. Cook and stir for 2 to 3 minutes or until mushrooms are tender. Stir in the remaining mustard mixture and orange juice. Cook and stir until heated through.

5 To serve, thinly slice the meat. Spoon the mushroom mixture over meat.

Nutrition facts per serving: 240 cal., 4 g total fat (1 g sat. fat), 60 mg chol., 334 mg sodium, 32 g carbo., 21 g pro.

chicken FINGERS WITH HONEY SAUCE

Serve your favorite barbecue sauce as a quick alternative to the honey sauce.

Start to Finish: 20 minutes
Bake: 11 minutes
Makes: 4 servings

12 ounces skinless, boneless chicken breast halves

2 egg whites, slightly beaten

1 tablespoon honey

2 cups cornflakes, crushed

¼ teaspoon ground black pepper

¼ cup honey

4 teaspoons mustard or Dijon-style mustard

¼ teaspoon garlic powder

1 Preheat oven to 450°F. Cut chicken into 3×¾-inch strips. In a small bowl, combine egg whites and the 1 tablespoon honey. In a shallow dish, combine crushed cornflakes and pepper. Dip chicken strips in egg white mixture and roll in cornflake mixture to coat.

2 Place chicken in a single layer on an ungreased baking sheet. Bake for 11 to 13 minutes or until chicken is no longer pink.

3 Meanwhile, for sauce, in a small bowl stir together the ¼ cup honey, the mustard, and garlic powder. Serve the chicken strips with sauce.

Nutrition facts per serving: 230 cal., 2 g total fat (1 g sat. fat), 45 mg chol., 275 mg sodium, 31 g carbo., 19 g pro.

curried CHICKEN THIGHS

You also can use skinless, boneless chicken thighs in this Indian-style recipe. Just reduce the cooking time to 10 minutes after adding the chicken broth.

Prep: 20 minutes
Cook: 25 minutes
Makes: 4 servings

- 8 **chicken thighs (about 2½ pounds total)**
- 2 **tablespoons cooking oil**
- 1 **cup sliced fresh mushrooms**
- 1 **medium onion, chopped (½ cup)**
- 1 **clove garlic, minced**
- 3 **to 4 teaspoons curry powder**
- ¼ **teaspoon salt**
- ¼ **teaspoon ground cinnamon**
- ¾ **cup chicken broth**
- 1 **medium apple, cored and chopped**
- 1 **cup half-and-half, light cream, or milk**
- 2 **tablespoons all-purpose flour**
- 3 **cups hot cooked rice**
- **Assorted condiments: raisins, chopped hard-cooked egg, peanuts, chopped tomato, chopped green sweet pepper, toasted coconut, chutney, cut-up fruits (optional)**

1 Skin chicken. Rinse chicken; pat dry with paper towels. In a 10-inch skillet, cook chicken in hot oil over medium heat for about 10 minutes or until lightly browned, turning to brown evenly. Remove chicken. If necessary, add 1 tablespoon additional cooking oil to skillet.

2 Add mushrooms, onion, and garlic to skillet; cook until vegetables are tender. Add curry powder, salt, and cinnamon; cook and stir for 1 minute. Add chicken broth and apple. Return chicken to skillet. Bring to boiling; reduce heat. Cover and simmer for about 15 minutes or until chicken is tender and no longer pink.

3 Transfer chicken to platter; keep warm. Stir the half-and-half, light cream, or milk into the flour. Stir into pan juices. Cook and stir until thickened and bubbly. Cook and stir for 1 minute more. Spoon some sauce over chicken. Pass remaining sauce. Serve with rice and, if desired, pass condiments.

Nutrition facts per serving: 695 cal., 32 g total fat (10 g sat. fat), 158 mg chol., 829 mg sodium, 45 g carbo., 54 g pro.

quick CHICKEN MOLE

Declare a Mexican theme night by serving this dish with warm flour tortillas, tomato salsa seasoned with snipped fresh cilantro, and sliced oranges layered with coconut for dessert.

Prep: 15 minutes
Cook: 30 minutes
Makes: 6 servings

- 6 **medium chicken breast halves (about 3 pounds total)**
- 2 **tablespoons olive oil or cooking oil**
- 1 **small onion, chopped**
- 1½ **teaspoons chili powder**
- 1 **teaspoon sesame seeds**
- 1 **clove garlic, minced**
- ¼ **teaspoon salt**
- ¼ **teaspoon ground cumin**
- ¼ **teaspoon ground cinnamon**
- 1 **small tomato, chopped**
- 1 **tomatillo, peeled and cut into wedges, or 1 small tomato, chopped**
- ½ **cup chicken broth**
- ½ **cup tomato sauce**
- 2 **tablespoons raisins**
- 2 **teaspoons unsweetened cocoa powder**
- **Several dashes bottled hot pepper sauce**
- **Hot cooked rice**
- **Pumpkin seeds or slivered almonds, toasted (optional)**

1 Skin chicken. In a large skillet, cook chicken in hot oil over medium heat for about 10 minutes or until light brown, turning to brown evenly. Add onion, chili powder, sesame seeds, garlic, salt, cumin, and cinnamon. Cook and stir for 30 seconds.

2 Stir in tomato, tomatillo, chicken broth, tomato sauce, raisins, cocoa powder, and hot pepper sauce. Bring to boiling; reduce heat. Simmer, uncovered, about 15 minutes or until chicken is no longer pink (170°F). Using a slotted spoon, remove chicken pieces from skillet. Simmer the tomato mixture, uncovered, for 4 to 5 minutes or to desired consistency.

3 To serve, spoon tomato mixture over chicken and rice. If desired, sprinkle with pumpkin seeds or almonds.

Nutrition facts per serving: 367 cal., 9 g total fat (2 g sat. fat), 76 mg chol., 543 mg sodium, 37 g carbo., 33 g pro.

Garlic Hints

Working with garlic is easy if you know how to handle it. Loosen the garlic skin quickly by crushing each clove with the flat side of a chef's knife. The skin will slip off. To mince the peeled garlic, place it in a garlic press or use a sharp knife to cut it into tiny pieces. If you prefer, use bottled minced garlic (usually found in your supermarket's produce section) instead of the cloves.

pollo RELLENO

Expect oohs and aahs when you serve these chicken rolls; each has a cheese-stuffed chile pepper inside.

Prep: 20 minutes
Bake: 25 minutes
Makes: 6 servings

6 medium skinless, boneless chicken breast halves (about 1½ pounds total)

⅓ cup yellow cornmeal

½ of a 1¼-ounce package (2 tablespoons) taco seasoning mix

1 egg

1 4-ounce can whole green chile peppers, rinsed, seeded, and cut in half lengthwise (6 pieces total)

2 ounces Monterey Jack cheese, cut into six 2×½-inch sticks

2 tablespoons snipped fresh cilantro or parsley

¼ teaspoon ground black pepper

¼ teaspoon crushed red pepper

1 8-ounce jar taco sauce or salsa

½ cup shredded Monterey Jack or cheddar cheese (optional)

Fresh cilantro sprigs (optional)

1 Preheat oven to 375°F. Place each chicken piece between two pieces of plastic wrap. Pound lightly with the flat side of a meat mallet until about ⅛ inch thick. Remove plastic wrap.

2 In a shallow bowl, combine cornmeal and taco seasoning mix. Place egg in another shallow bowl; beat lightly.

3 For each chicken roll, place a chile pepper half on a chicken piece near an edge. Place a cheese stick on top of chile pepper. Sprinkle with some of the snipped cilantro or parsley, black pepper, and red pepper. Fold in sides; starting from edge with cheese, roll up chicken.

4 Dip chicken rolls into egg and roll in cornmeal mixture to coat. Place rolls, seam sides down, in a shallow baking pan. Bake for 25 to 30 minutes or until chicken is no longer pink.

5 Heat taco sauce or salsa. If desired, sprinkle chicken rolls with shredded cheese. Serve with taco sauce or salsa. If desired, garnish with cilantro sprigs.

Nutrition facts per serving: 235 cal., 10 g total fat (3 g sat. fat), 103 mg chol., 769 mg sodium, 13 g carbo., 28 g pro.

thyme CHICKEN MARSALA

Start to Finish: 30 minutes
Makes: 2 servings

2 medium skinless, boneless chicken breast halves (about 10 ounces total)

Salt

Ground black pepper

1 tablespoon all-purpose flour

2 tablespoons olive oil

1 medium carrot, cut into thin, bite-size strips (½ cup)

1 small red or yellow sweet pepper, cut into thin, bite-size strips

2 cloves garlic, minced

¼ teaspoon salt

¼ teaspoon ground black pepper

⅓ cup dry Marsala

1 tablespoon snipped fresh thyme

Hot cooked linguine (optional)

1 Place each chicken piece between two pieces of plastic wrap. Working from the center to the edges, pound lightly with the flat side of a meat mallet until ¼ inch thick. Remove plastic wrap. Sprinkle chicken lightly with salt and pepper. Coat the chicken with flour, shaking off excess. Set aside.

2 In a large skillet, heat 1 tablespoon of the oil over medium heat. Add carrot strips; cook and stir for 3 minutes. Add sweet pepper strips, garlic, salt, and black pepper; cook and stir for 4 to 5 minutes or until vegetables are crisp-tender. Divide the vegetable mixture between two dinner plates. Cover and keep warm.

3 In the same skillet, heat the remaining 1 tablespoon oil. Add chicken. Cook for 4 to 5 minutes or until chicken is tender and no longer pink, turning once. Place the chicken on top of cooked vegetables.

4 Add Marsala and thyme to skillet. Scrape up any browned bits from the bottom of the skillet. Spoon Marsala mixture over chicken. If desired, serve with linguine.

Nutrition facts per serving: 354 cal., 16 g total fat (3 g sat. fat), 82 mg chol., 555 mg sodium, 11 g carbo., 34 g pro.

chicken AND PROSCIUTTO ROLL-UPS

This pretty dish takes the Italian technique braciola—wrapping thin slices of meat around savories such as Italian ham, cheese, artichokes, spinach, and herbs—and applies it to chicken. Serve these attractive spirals with spinach fettuccine.

Prep: 20 minutes
Grill: 15 minutes
Makes: 4 servings

¼ **cup dry white wine**

2 **teaspoons snipped fresh thyme or ½ teaspoon dried thyme, crushed**

4 **medium skinless, boneless chicken breast halves (about 1 pound total)**

4 **thin slices prosciutto (about 1 ounce total), trimmed of fat**

2 **ounces fontina cheese, thinly sliced**

½ **of a 7-ounce jar roasted red sweet peppers, cut into thin strips (about ½ cup)**

Fresh thyme sprigs (optional)

1 For sauce, in a small bowl combine wine and the snipped fresh or dried thyme. Set aside.

2 Place each chicken piece between two pieces of plastic wrap. Pound lightly with the flat side of a meat mallet until about ⅛ inch thick. Remove plastic wrap.

3 For each chicken roll, place a slice of prosciutto and one-quarter of the cheese on a chicken piece near an edge. Arrange one-quarter of the roasted pepper strips on top of cheese. Fold in the sides; starting from edge with pepper strips, roll up chicken. Secure with wooden toothpicks. (If desired, wrap each chicken roll in plastic wrap and chill for up to 4 hours.)

4 Place chicken rolls on the rack of an uncovered grill directly over medium coals. Grill for 15 to 17 minutes or until chicken is no longer pink, turning to cook evenly and brushing twice with sauce. Remove the toothpicks. If desired, garnish chicken rolls with fresh thyme sprigs.

Nutrition facts per serving: 214 cal., 9 g total fat (4 g sat. fat), 76 mg chol., 294 mg sodium, 2 g carbo., 27 g pro.

chicken AND MUSHROOMS

Whether to slice the mushrooms or not depends on their size. If they're larger than 1½ inches in diameter, slice them. Otherwise leave them whole.

Prep: 30 minutes
Cook: 20 minutes
Makes: 4 to 6 servings

4 chicken thighs

4 chicken drumsticks

¼ cup all-purpose flour

¼ teaspoon salt

¼ teaspoon ground black pepper

¼ teaspoon paprika

2 tablespoons cooking oil

2 cups whole or sliced fresh mushrooms

1 medium red sweet pepper, cut into 1-inch strips

1 medium onion, sliced

3 cloves garlic, minced

½ cup dry red wine or beef broth

2 tablespoons balsamic vinegar

1 14.5-ounce can diced tomatoes

2 teaspoons dried Italian seasoning, crushed

¼ cup half-and-half or light cream

1 tablespoon all-purpose flour

Hot cooked pasta (optional)

¼ cup snipped fresh parsley

1 Skin chicken. In a large self-sealing plastic bag, combine the ¼ cup flour, the salt, pepper, and paprika. Add 2 or 3 pieces of chicken to the bag at a time. Seal and shake to coat well.

2 In a very large skillet, heat the oil over medium heat. Cook the chicken in hot oil for 10 to 15 minutes or until brown, turning to brown evenly. Remove chicken from skillet, reserving drippings in skillet.

3 Add mushrooms, sweet pepper, onion, and garlic to the reserved drippings in skillet. Cook and stir for 2 minutes. Add red wine or beef broth and balsamic vinegar. Cook and stir for 5 minutes more. Stir in undrained tomatoes and Italian seasoning.

4 Bring to boiling, scraping up any browned bits on bottom of skillet. Return chicken to skillet; reduce heat. Cover and simmer about 20 minutes or until chicken is no longer pink (180°F). Remove chicken; cover and keep warm.

5 Stir together half-and-half or light cream and the 1 tablespoon flour; stir into tomato mixture. Cook and stir until slightly thickened and bubbly. Cook and stir for 1 minute more. Return chicken to skillet; heat through. If desired, serve over hot cooked pasta. Sprinkle with parsley.

Nutrition facts per serving: 323 cal., 13 g total fat (3 g sat. fat), 89 mg chol., 400 mg sodium, 21 g carbo., 25 g pro.

curried COCONUT SHRIMP

Start to Finish: 30 minutes
Makes: 4 servings

1 **pound fresh or frozen large shrimp in shells, thawed (14 to 16 count)**

1 **cup uncooked jasmine rice**

1 **15.25-ounce can tropical fruit salad or pineapple chunks**

1 **teaspoon red curry paste**

1 **cup unsweetened coconut milk**

1 Thaw shrimp, if frozen. Prepare rice according to package directions; set aside. Meanwhile, peel and devein shrimp. Rinse shrimp; pat dry with paper towels; set aside. Drain liquid from fruit, reserving ½ cup. Set liquid and fruit aside.

2 In a large nonstick skillet, stir-fry shrimp and curry paste over medium-high heat for 3 to 4 minutes or until shrimp are opaque. Remove shrimp from skillet; set aside. Add coconut milk and reserved liquid from fruit to skillet. Bring to boiling; reduce heat. Simmer, uncovered, for 5 to 7 minutes until mixture is slightly thickened and reduced to about 1 cup.

3 Divide hot cooked rice among four shallow bowls. Arrange shrimp on top of rice; spoon sauce over shrimp and rice. Top each serving with ¼ cup drained fruit.

Nutrition facts per serving: 463 cal., 17 g total fat (13 g sat. fat), 151 mg chol., 263 mg sodium, 55 g carbo., 24 g pro.

shrimp PICCATA

Lemon, garlic, and white wine characterize this exceptionally easy, yet oh-so-elegant, entrée. Accompany the meal with crisp-tender stalks of steamed asparagus and garnish with scored lemon slices.

Start to Finish: 25 minutes
Makes: 4 servings

1 **pound fresh or frozen large shrimp, peeled and deveined**
2 **tablespoons all-purpose flour**
⅓ **cup dry white wine**
2 **tablespoons lemon juice**
1 **tablespoon capers, drained**
¼ **teaspoon salt**
⅛ **teaspoon ground black pepper**
1 **tablespoon margarine or butter**
2 **cloves garlic, minced**
2 **cups hot cooked brown rice and/or wild rice**
  Lemon slices, halved (optional)

1 Thaw shrimp, if frozen. Rinse shrimp; pat dry with paper towels. In a medium bowl, toss shrimp with flour until coated. Set aside.

2 For sauce, in a small bowl stir together wine, lemon juice, capers, salt, and pepper. Set aside.

3 Place margarine or butter in a wok or large skillet. Preheat over medium-high heat until margarine is melted (add more margarine if necessary during cooking). Stir-fry garlic in hot margarine for 15 seconds.

4 Add half of the shrimp to wok. Stir-fry for 2 to 3 minutes or until shrimp turn opaque. Remove from wok. Repeat with the remaining shrimp. Remove all shrimp from wok.

5 Add sauce to wok. Cook and stir until sauce is bubbly and slightly reduced. Return shrimp to wok. Cook and stir for about 1 minute more or until heated through.

6 Serve immediately over hot cooked brown and/or wild rice. If desired, garnish with lemon slices.

Nutrition facts per serving: 247 cal., 4 g total fat (1 g sat. fat), 174 mg chol., 405 mg sodium, 27 g carbo., 21 g pro.

stir-fried SHRIMP AND BROCCOLI

This pleasing mixture of broccoli, carrots, and seasonings tastes equally delicious with shrimp or scallops. If you prefer, leave the tails on the shrimp for a striking presentation.

Start to Finish: 25 minutes
Makes: 4 servings

- 1 **pound fresh or frozen medium shrimp in shells or 12 ounces fresh or frozen scallops**
- 3 **tablespoons red wine vinegar**
- 3 **tablespoons soy sauce**
- 3 **tablespoons water**
- 1 **tablespoon cornstarch**
- 1½ **teaspoons sugar**
- 1 **tablespoon cooking oil**
- 2 **cloves garlic, minced**
- 2 **cups broccoli florets**
- 1 **cup thinly bias-sliced carrots**
- 1 **small onion, halved lengthwise and sliced**
- 1 **cup sliced fresh mushrooms**
- 2 **cups hot cooked vermicelli, fusilli, or rice**

1 Thaw shrimp or scallops, if frozen. Peel and devein shrimp or cut any large scallops in half. Rinse the shrimp or scallops; pat dry with paper towels. Set aside.

2 For sauce, in a small bowl combine vinegar, soy sauce, water, cornstarch, and sugar; set aside.

3 Add oil to a wok or large skillet. Preheat over medium-high heat (add more oil if necessary during cooking). Stir-fry garlic in hot oil for 15 seconds. Add broccoli, carrots, and onion. Stir-fry for 3 minutes. Add mushrooms; stir-fry for 1 to 2 minutes more or until vegetables are crisp-tender. Remove vegetables from wok.

4 Stir sauce; add to wok. Bring to boiling. Add shrimp or scallops and cook for 2 to 3 minutes or until shrimp or scallops turn opaque. Return cooked vegetables to wok. Stir all ingredients together to coat. Heat through. Serve immediately with hot cooked pasta or rice.

Nutrition facts per serving: 395 cal., 6 g total fat (1 g sat. fat), 131 mg chol., 968 mg sodium, 62 g carbo., 26 g pro.

salmon WITH DIJON-CREAM SAUCE

Start to Finish: 25 minutes
Makes: 4 servings

1¼ **pounds fresh or frozen skinless salmon fillets**

 1 **tablespoon butter**

⅓ **cup reduced-sodium chicken broth**

⅓ **cup half-and-half or light cream**

 2 **tablespoons Dijon-style mustard**

¼ **teaspoon coarsely ground black pepper**

1 Thaw fish, if frozen. Rinse fish; pat dry with paper towels. Cut fillets crosswise into ½-inch slices. In a large skillet, cook salmon slices, half at a time, in hot butter over medium-high heat for about 2 minutes or until fish begins to flake when tested with a fork, turning once. Remove from skillet; keep warm.

2 For sauce, add chicken broth to drippings in skillet. Bring to boiling; reduce heat. Simmer, uncovered, for 1 minute. Whisk together half-and-half and mustard; stir into skillet. Return to boiling; reduce heat. Simmer, uncovered, for 2 to 3 minutes more or until sauce is slightly thickened. Spoon sauce over salmon; sprinkle with pepper.

Nutrition facts per serving: 318 cal., 20 g total fat (6 g sat. fat), 95 mg chol., 343 mg sodium, 1 g carbo., 29 g pro.

parmesan BAKED FISH

Start to Finish: 22 minutes
Oven: 450°F
Makes: 4 servings

4 4- to 5-ounce fresh or frozen skinless salmon or other firm fish fillets, ¾ to 1 inch thick

¼ cup mayonnaise or salad dressing

2 tablespoons grated Parmesan cheese

1 tablespoon snipped fresh chives

1 teaspoon Worcestershire sauce for chicken

1 Thaw fish, if frozen. Preheat oven to 450°F. Rinse fish; pat dry with paper towels. Place fish in a greased 2-quart baking dish, tucking under any thin edges to make fish uniform thickness.

2 In a small bowl, stir together mayonnaise, Parmesan cheese, chives, and Worcestershire sauce. Spread mixture evenly over fish. Bake, uncovered, for 12 to 15 minutes or until fish begins to flake when tested with a fork.

Nutrition facts per serving: 302 cal., 22 g total fat (4 g sat. fat), 77 mg chol., 185 mg sodium, 0 g carbo., 25 g pro.

sesame ORANGE ROUGHY

To make onion brushes, slice roots from the end of each green onion and remove most of the upper green portion. Slash the remaining green portion to make a fringe. Then place in ice water for a few minutes to curl the ends.

Start to Finish: 25 minutes
Makes: 4 servings

1 **pound fresh or frozen orange roughy or other fish fillets, about ¾ inch thick**

2 **tablespoons lime or lemon juice**

1 **tablespoon margarine or butter**

2 **tablespoons water**

4 **teaspoons soy sauce**

2 **teaspoons honey**

1 **clove garlic, minced**

½ **teaspoon grated fresh ginger or ⅛ teaspoon ground ginger**

½ **teaspoon toasted sesame oil**

½ **teaspoon lime or lemon juice**

¼ **teaspoon ground black pepper**

1 **green onion, sliced**

2 **teaspoons sesame seeds, toasted**

1 Thaw fish, if frozen. Rinse fish; pat dry with paper towels. Cut fish into serving-size portions. Brush both sides of fish with the 2 tablespoons lime or lemon juice.

2 In a large skillet, cook fish in hot margarine or butter over medium heat for 6 to 9 minutes or until fish flakes easily with a fork, turning once. Transfer fish to dinner plates; cover and keep warm.

3 Meanwhile, in a small bowl combine water, soy sauce, honey, garlic, ginger, sesame oil, the ½ teaspoon juice, and the pepper. Carefully pour into skillet. Cook until heated through, scraping up any browned bits on bottom. Pour over fish. Sprinkle with green onion and sesame seeds.

Nutrition facts per serving: 269 cal., 5 g total fat (1 g sat. fat), 23 mg chol., 453 mg sodium, 33 g carbo., 21 g pro.

Thawing Fish

Your best bet for safety and quality is to thaw fish and shellfish slowly in the refrigerator. Place the unopened package of fish or shellfish in a container in the refrigerator and allow overnight thawing for a 1-pound package. If necessary, you can place the wrapped package under cold running water for 1 to 2 minutes to hasten thawing. Don't thaw fish or shellfish in warm water or at room temperature and do not refreeze fish; doing so is unsafe.

sandwiches
AND WRAPS

Salmon and Asparagus Wraps, *recipe page 132*

mustard STEAK SANDWICHES

Save calories by serving this sandwich with just the bottom half of the roll. Use a knife and fork for easier eating.

Prep: 10 minutes
Broil: 15 minutes
Makes: 6 servings

2 tablespoons Dijon-style mustard

1 teaspoon brown sugar

½ teaspoon cracked black pepper

1 clove garlic, minced

1 pound beef flank steak, trimmed of fat

3 hoagie rolls, split and toasted

1 cup shredded lettuce

   Thinly sliced tomato

   Dijon-style mustard (optional)

1 In a small bowl, stir together mustard, brown sugar, pepper, and garlic. Set aside.

2 Place meat on the unheated rack of a broiler pan. Score steak on both sides by making shallow cuts at 1-inch intervals in a diamond pattern. Brush steak with some of the mustard mixture. Broil steak 4 to 5 inches from the heat for 7 minutes. Turn and brush steak with remaining mustard mixture. Broil until done as desired, allowing 8 to 11 minutes more for medium (160°F).

3 To serve, thinly slice meat diagonally across the grain. Top each hoagie half with some of the lettuce and sliced tomato. Layer meat slices on each sandwich. If desired, serve with additional mustard.

Nutrition facts per serving: 333 cal., 9 g total fat (3 g sat. fat), 30 mg chol., 500 mg sodium, 38 g carbo., 22 g pro.

Fatless Flavor

It's no secret that fat, salt, and sugar give food flavor, so when it comes to eating healthfully, replacing these things with other ingredients is important. Certainly ingredients like mustard, pepper, vinegar, and salsa are great low-cal, fat-free flavorings. And there are so many varieties of each of these that the possibilities are endless. Consider hot or honey mustard, balsamic or raspberry vinegar, and tomato or black bean salsa. The list goes on. As long as you're willing to experiment, you'll never run out of variations.

five-spice STEAK WRAPS

Start to Finish: 25 minutes
Makes: 4 servings

12 ounces boneless beef round steak

2 cups packaged coleslaw mix

¼ cup red and/or green sweet pepper cut into thin, bite-size strips

¼ cup carrot cut into thin, bite-size strips

¼ cup snipped fresh chives

2 tablespoons rice vinegar

½ teaspoon toasted sesame oil

½ teaspoon five-spice powder

¼ teaspoon salt

Nonstick cooking spray

¼ cup plain low-fat yogurt or light dairy sour cream

4 8-inch flour tortillas

1 If desired, partially freeze steak for easier slicing. In a medium bowl, combine coleslaw mix, sweet pepper, carrot, and chives. In a small bowl, combine vinegar and sesame oil. Pour vinegar mixture over coleslaw mixture; toss to coat. Set aside.

2 Trim fat from steak. Thinly slice steak across the grain into bite-size strips. Sprinkle strips with five-spice powder and salt. Lightly coat an unheated large nonstick skillet with nonstick cooking spray. Preheat over medium-high heat. Add steak strips; stir-fry for 3 to 4 minutes or until brown.

3 Spread 1 tablespoon of the yogurt down the center of each tortilla. Top with steak strips. Stir coleslaw mixture; spoon over steak. Fold in sides of tortillas. If desired, secure with wooden toothpicks.

Nutrition facts per serving: 237 cal., 7 g total fat (2 g sat. fat), 51 mg chol., 329 mg sodium, 20 g carbo., 22 g pro.

beef AND CABBAGE WRAPS

Start to Finish: 20 minutes
Oven: 350°F
Makes: 4 servings

- 8 8-inch flour tortillas
- 12 ounces lean ground beef
- ½ cup chopped onion (1 medium)
- 1 clove garlic, minced
- 1 cup whole kernel corn
- ½ to ⅔ cup bottled barbecue sauce
- 2 cups packaged coleslaw mix

1 Preheat oven to 350°F. Wrap tortillas in foil; place on a baking sheet. Heat for 10 minutes or until heated through.

2 Meanwhile, in a large skillet, cook beef, onion, and garlic over medium heat until beef is brown and onion is tender. Drain off fat. Stir in corn and ⅓ cup of the barbecue sauce. Cook and stir until heated through.

3 To serve, spread one side of each tortilla with some of the remaining barbecue sauce. Spoon about ½ cup filling on each tortilla. Top with some of the coleslaw mix. Roll up.

Nutrition facts per serving: 391 cal., 14 g total fat (4 g sat. fat), 54 mg chol., 535 mg sodium, 46 g carbo., 21 g pro.

island REUBENS

Prep: 10 minutes
Broil: 5 minutes
Makes: 4 servings

- 8 slices dark rye bread, toasted
- ½ cup bottled Thousand Island salad dressing
- 6 ounces sliced cooked turkey
- 6 ounces sliced cooked ham
- 4 slices Swiss cheese
- 1 cup canned sauerkraut, well drained
- ½ cup canned crushed pineapple, well drained
- 4 slices sharp cheddar cheese
- 4 slices red onion

1 Place bread slices on an extra-large baking sheet. Spread one side of each slice with salad dressing. Top half of the bread slices with turkey, ham, and Swiss cheese. Top remaining bread slices with sauerkraut, crushed pineapple, cheese, and onion.

2 Broil 5 inches from the heat for 5 minutes or until cheese melts. Carefully top turkey-topped bread slices with sauerkraut-topped slices, onion side down.

Nutrition facts per serving: 677 cal., 36 g total fat (15 g sat. fat), 120 mg chol., 2,948 mg sodium, 44 g carbo., 40 g pro.

egg AND VEGETABLE WRAPS

Need a lunchtime energy boost? High-protein eggs wrapped with crisp, refreshing veggies with a light dressing are the perfect solution.

Start to Finish: 30 minutes
Makes: 6 servings

- 4 hard-cooked eggs, chopped
- 1 cup chopped cucumber
- 1 cup chopped zucchini or yellow summer squash
- ½ cup finely chopped red onion
- ½ cup shredded carrot
- ¼ cup fat-free or light mayonnaise dressing or salad dressing
- 2 tablespoons Dijon-style mustard
- 1 tablespoon fat-free milk
- 1 teaspoon snipped fresh tarragon or basil
- ⅛ teaspoon paprika
- 6 lettuce leaves
- 6 10-inch whole wheat, spinach, or vegetable flour tortillas
- 2 roma tomatoes, thinly sliced

1 In a large bowl, combine eggs, cucumber, zucchini, red onion, and carrot. For dressing, in a small bowl stir together mayonnaise dressing, Dijon mustard, milk, tarragon, and paprika. Pour dressing over the egg mixture; toss gently to coat.

2 For each sandwich, place a lettuce leaf on a tortilla. Place 3 or 4 tomato slices on top of the lettuce, slightly off center. Spoon about ⅔ cup of the egg mixture on top of the tomato slices. Fold in two opposite sides of the tortilla; roll up from the bottom. Cut the rolls in half diagonally.

Nutrition facts per serving: 265 cal., 7 g total fat (2 g sat. fat), 141 mg chol., 723 mg sodium, 40 g carbo., 11 g pro.

peppery ARTICHOKE PITAS

These pitas are filled with ingredients you can keep on hand: canned artichokes, canned beans, and bottled garlic dressing. Keep the pantry stocked and you'll always have what you need to put a great meal on the table.

Start to Finish: 20 minutes
Makes: 6 servings

1   15-ounce can black-eyed peas, rinsed and drained

1   13.75- to 14-ounce can artichoke hearts, drained and cut up

1   cup torn mixed salad greens

¼   cup bottled creamy garlic salad dressing

¼   teaspoon cracked black pepper

3   pita bread rounds, halved crosswise

1   small tomato, sliced

1 In a medium bowl, combine black-eyed peas, artichoke hearts, mixed greens, salad dressing, and pepper. Line pita bread halves with tomato slices. Spoon artichoke mixture into pita bread halves.

Nutrition facts per serving: 189 cal., 4 g total fat (1 g sat. fat), 0 mg chol., 632 mg sodium, 31 g carbo., 7 g pro.

stuffed FOCACCIA

Start to Finish: 20 minutes
Makes: 3 servings

½ of a 9- to 10-inch garlic, onion, or plain Italian flatbread (focaccia), split horizontally

½ of an 8-ounce container mascarpone cheese

1 6-ounce jar marinated artichoke hearts, drained and chopped

1 tablespoon capers, drained (optional)

4 ounces thinly sliced Genoa salami

1 cup arugula leaves

1 Spread cut sides of focaccia with mascarpone cheese. Sprinkle bottom half of focaccia with artichoke hearts and, if desired, capers. Top with salami and arugula leaves. Cover with top of focaccia, spread side down.

2 Cut sandwich into thirds. Serve immediately or wrap and chill for up to 4 hours.

Nutrition facts per serving: 545 cal., 36 g total fat (16 g sat. fat), 83 mg chol., 970 mg sodium, 43 g carbo., 23 g pro.

lahvosh ROLL

Lahvosh looks and feels like a giant crisp cracker, and you must soften it before using. (You may be able to find the presoftened variety and skip step 1.)

Prep: 15 minutes
Stand: 1 hour
Chill: 2 hours
Makes: 6 servings

1 **15-inch sesame seed lahvosh (Armenian cracker bread) or two 10-inch tortillas**

½ **of an 8-ounce tub cream cheese with chives and onion**

¼ **cup chopped marinated artichoke hearts, drained**

2 **tablespoons diced pimiento**

1 **teaspoon dried oregano, crushed**

6 **ounces thinly sliced prosciutto or cooked ham**

4 **ounces sliced provolone cheese**

2 **large romaine lettuce leaves, ribs removed**

① Dampen both sides of lahvosh by holding it briefly under gently running cold water. Place lahvosh, seeded side down, between two damp, clean kitchen towels. Let stand for about 1 hour or until soft.

② In a bowl, stir together cream cheese, artichoke hearts, pimiento, and oregano. Remove top towel from lahvosh. Spread lahvosh with cream cheese filling. Arrange prosciutto over cream cheese. Place provolone slices in center and lettuce next to provolone. Roll from lettuce edge, using the towel to lift and roll the bread. (Or, if using tortillas, spread tortillas with cream cheese mixture. Divide remaining ingredients between the tortillas. Roll up tortillas.)

③ Wrap roll in plastic wrap and chill seam side down for at least 2 hours. To serve, cut roll into 1-inch slices.

Nutrition facts per serving: 300 cal., 16 g total fat (8 g sat. fat), 51 mg chol., 1,226 mg sodium, 22 g carbo., 17 g pro.

Make Ahead Directions: Prepare Lahvosh Roll as directed through step 2. Wrap roll in plastic wrap and chill in the refrigerator seam side down for up to 24 hours. To serve, cut roll into 1-inch slices.

hawaiian TURKEY BURGERS

These unusual burgers are even better served with pineapple spritzers. Simply pour unsweetened pineapple juice over ice, filling a tall glass about one-third full, and top with carbonated water.

Prep: 20 minutes
Grill: 14 minutes
Makes: 4 servings

- **1 egg, beaten**
- **¼ cup seasoned fine dry bread crumbs**
- **3 tablespoons chopped water chestnuts**
- **¾ teaspoon ground ginger**
- **¼ teaspoon salt**
- **¼ teaspoon ground black pepper**
- **1 pound ground turkey or chicken**
- **¼ cup bottled sweet-and-sour sauce**
- **4 canned pineapple rings**
  Shredded spinach
- **4 kaiser rolls or hamburger buns, split and toasted**

1 In a medium bowl, combine egg, bread crumbs, water chestnuts, ginger, salt, and pepper. Add ground turkey or chicken; mix well. Form into four ¾-inch-thick patties.

2 Place patties on the rack of an uncovered grill directly over medium coals. Grill for 14 to 18 minutes or until done (165°F), turning once and brushing with sweet-and-sour sauce in the last 5 minutes of grilling. Meanwhile, place pineapple slices on grill rack. Grill for 5 minutes, turning occasionally.

3 To serve, place shredded spinach on the bottoms of rolls or buns. Top with burgers. Brush the burgers with sweet-and-sour sauce and top with pineapple slices. Replace roll or bun tops.

Nutrition facts per serving: 331 cal., 9 g total fat (2 g sat. fat), 108 mg chol., 1,092 mg sodium, 37 g carbo., 23 g pro.

team FAVORITE TURKEY BURGER

Prep: 15 minutes
Broil: 14 minutes
Makes: 4 servings

¼ cup fine dry bread crumbs

3 tablespoons ketchup

4 teaspoons dill or sweet pickle relish

½ teaspoon bottled minced garlic

¼ teaspoon salt

¼ teaspoon ground black pepper

1 pound ground turkey or chicken

⅓ cup low-fat mayonnaise dressing or salad dressing

4 romaine or green leaf lettuce leaves

8 tomato slices

4 whole wheat hamburger buns, split and toasted

1 Preheat broiler. In a large bowl, combine bread crumbs, 2 tablespoons ketchup, 2 teaspoons relish, garlic, salt, and ⅛ teaspoon pepper. Add ground turkey; mix well. Shape turkey mixture into four ¾-inch-thick patties.

2 In a small bowl, combine mayonnaise dressing, remaining 1 tablespoon ketchup, remaining 2 teaspoons relish, and remaining ⅛ teaspoon pepper; set aside.

3 Place patties on the unheated rack of a broiler pan. Broil 4 to 5 inches from the heat for 14 to 18 minutes or until no longer pink (165°F), turning once halfway through broiling. Place lettuce and tomato slices on the bottom halves of buns. Top with burgers. Spoon mayonnaise mixture on burgers. Add top halves of buns.

Nutrition facts per serving: 343 cal., 12 g total fat (3 g sat. fat), 74 mg chol., 953 mg sodium, 33 g carbo., 29 g pro.

turkey-tomato WRAPS

A cool idea for meals on the move, wraps are easy to pack and neat to eat.

Prep: 20 minutes
Chill: 2 hours
Makes: 6 servings

1   **7-ounce container prepared hummus**

3   **8- to 10-inch tomato-basil flour tortillas or plain flour tortillas**

8   **ounces thinly sliced, cooked peppered turkey breast**

6   **romaine lettuce leaves, ribs removed**

3   **small tomatoes, thinly sliced**

3   **thin slices red onion, separated into rings**

1 Spread hummus evenly over tortillas. Layer turkey breast, romaine, tomatoes, and onion on top of each tortilla. Roll up each tortilla into a spiral. Cut each roll in half and wrap with plastic wrap. Chill for 2 to 4 hours.

Nutrition facts per serving: 236 cal., 6 g total fat (1 g sat. fat), 32 mg chol., 458 mg sodium, 29 g carbo., 19 g pro.

Brown-Bagging It

Packing your own lunches for work is an easy way to eat healthier and saves money. Pack your lunch the night before so you can grab-and-go in the a.m. Be creative when putting your midday meal together. Wraps are great alternatives to sandwiches. Or skip the bread altogether and make roll-ups with lean meats and cheese. Try sprinkling dried cranberries into a salad with some slices of smoked turkey. Whatever you choose to put in your brown bag, be sure to use cold packs, if necessary, to keep your lunch at the correct temperature.

crunchy CURRIED CHICKEN SALAD WRAPS

Start to Finish: 20 minutes
Makes: 4 servings

- **4 10-inch flour tortillas**
- **1 9-ounce package frozen cooked chicken breast strips, thawed**
- **⅓ cup mayonnaise or salad dressing**
- **1½ teaspoons curry powder**
- **⅛ teaspoon ground black pepper**
- **1½ cups packaged coleslaw mix**
- **1 medium apple, cored and chopped**
- **½ cup pine nuts or slivered almonds, toasted (optional)**
- **⅓ cup fresh mint leaves, finely shredded**

1 Place tortillas on a flat surface; divide chicken among tortillas, placing near edge.

2 In a large bowl, combine mayonnaise, curry powder, and pepper. Add coleslaw mix, apple, pine nuts, if desired, and mint. Stir until well mixed. Spoon over chicken. Roll tortillas around filling; secure with wooden toothpicks, if necessary. Serve immediately or, if desired, wrap and chill for up to 24 hours.

Nutrition facts per wrap: 366 cal., 19 g total fat (4 g sat. fat), 44 mg chol., 329 mg sodium, 29 g carbo., 18 g pro.

chicken-veggie WRAPS

Start to Finish: 15 minutes
Makes: 4 servings

½ cup mayonnaise or salad dressing

3 to 4 tablespoons purchased sun-dried tomato pesto

12 6-inch corn tortillas or eight 7- to 8-inch flour tortillas

2 6-ounce packages refrigerated grilled chicken breast strips

2 small yellow summer squash or zucchini (8 ounces total), cut into thin strips

1 medium green sweet pepper, cut into strips

Fresh cilantro sprigs (optional)

1 Stir together mayonnaise and pesto; divide into four small bowls. Place tortillas on a microwave-safe plate, cover with a paper towel. Microwave on 100% power (high) for 30 to 45 seconds or until warm.

2 Divide chicken, squash and pepper strips, and warm tortillas among four shallow bowls. If desired, top with cilantro. Serve with pesto mixture.

Nutrition facts per serving: 481 cal., 30 g total fat (6 g sat. fat), 66 mg chol., 1,021 mg sodium, 30 g carbo., 24 g pro.

clam AND BACON BUNDLES

Brush the bundles with milk before you bake them; you'll be rewarded with a crispy, irresistibly golden brown crust.

Prep: 25 minutes
Bake: 20 minutes
Cool: 5 minutes
Makes: 4 servings

2   slices bacon, chopped

¾   cup finely chopped broccoli
    (4 to 5 ounces)

1   medium carrot, shredded
    (½ cup)

1   small yellow summer squash,
    chopped (1 cup)

2   6½-ounce cans chopped
    clams, drained

⅓   of an 8-ounce tub (⅓ cup)
    cream cheese with chives
    and onion

2   tablespoons bottled creamy
    cucumber salad dressing

1   10-ounce package
    refrigerated pizza dough

1   tablespoon milk

1   tablespoon sesame seeds

1 Preheat oven to 400°F. In a large skillet, cook bacon over medium heat until crisp. Drain bacon, reserving 1 tablespoon drippings in skillet. Set bacon aside.

2 For filling, add broccoli and carrot to the reserved drippings in skillet. Cook and stir for 2 minutes. Add squash; cook and stir for 1 minute more. Remove from heat. Stir in clams, cream cheese, cucumber salad dressing, and bacon.

3 Grease a baking sheet; set aside. On a lightly floured surface, roll pizza dough into a 12-inch square. Cut dough into four 6-inch squares. Place ½ cup of the filling on one corner of each square. Moisten edges and fold opposite corner over filling. Press edges with tines of a fork to seal. Brush bundles with milk. Sprinkle with sesame seeds.

4 Place bundles on the prepared baking sheet. Bake for about 20 minutes or until golden brown. Cool on a wire rack for 5 minutes. Serve warm.

Nutrition facts per serving: 390 cal., 18 g total fat (5 g sat. fat), 57 mg chol., 494 mg sodium, 35 g carbo., 23 g pro.

shrimp-avocado HOAGIES

Start to Finish: 20 minutes
Makes: 4 servings

1 **10- to 12-ounce package frozen peeled, cooked shrimp, thawed and chopped**

2 **large avocados, pitted, peeled, and chopped**

½ **cup packaged shredded carrots**

⅓ **cup bottled coleslaw salad dressing**

4 **hoagie buns**

Lemon wedges (optional)

1 In a large bowl, combine shrimp, avocados, carrots, and salad dressing.

2 Halve hoagie buns. Using a spoon, slightly hollow bottoms and tops of hoagie buns, leaving a ½-inch shell. Discard excess bread. Toast buns.

3 Spoon shrimp mixture into hoagie buns. If desired, serve with lemon wedges.

Nutrition facts per serving: 560 cal., 24 g total fat (4 g sat. fat), 144 mg chol., 825 mg sodium, 63 g carbo., 25 g pro.

salmon AND ASPARAGUS WRAPS

Start to Finish: 25 minutes
Makes: 4 servings

12 thin fresh asparagus spears (about 4 ounces)

½ cup cream cheese spread with chive and onion

2 teaspoons finely shredded lemon peel

2 tablespoons lemon juice

⅛ teaspoon cayenne pepper

6 ounces smoked salmon, flaked, skin and bones removed

4 6- to 7-inch whole wheat flour tortillas

2 tablespoons snipped fresh basil or 1 teaspoon dried basil, crushed

½ of a medium red sweet pepper, seeded and cut into thin, bite-size strips

1 Snap off and discard woody bases from asparagus. In a covered medium saucepan, cook asparagus spears in a small amount of boiling lightly salted water for 2 to 3 minutes or until crisp-tender. Drain; plunge into ice water to cool. Drain again; pat dry with paper towels.

2 In a medium bowl, stir together cream cheese, lemon peel, lemon juice, and cayenne pepper. Fold in flaked salmon. Spread on tortillas. Arrange basil, 3 asparagus spears, and one-quarter of the sweet pepper strips over salmon mixture on each tortilla. Roll up tortillas. If necessary, secure with toothpicks. Serve immediately or wrap in plastic wrap and chill for up to 6 hours.

Nutrition facts per serving: 223 cal., 14 g total fat (1 g sat. fat), 40 mg chol., 650 mg sodium, 16 g carbo., 15 g pro.

seasoned TUNA SANDWICHES

Tired of the same brown-bag lunch? This recipe combines an old favorite—tuna—with fruity olive oil, fresh lemon juice, and capers for a taste of the Mediterranean.

Start to Finish: 15 minutes
Makes: 4 servings

- 2 **6-ounce cans solid white tuna (water-pack), drained**
- 2 **tablespoons olive oil**
- 2 **teaspoons lemon juice**
- 1 **teaspoon capers, drained**
- ⅛ **teaspoon ground black pepper**
- 2 **tablespoons fat-free mayonnaise dressing or salad dressing**
- 8 **slices whole wheat bread**
- 4 **lettuce leaves (optional)**
- 4 **tomato slices**

1 In a small bowl, combine tuna, oil, lemon juice, capers, and pepper.

2 To assemble each sandwich, spread ½ tablespoon of the mayonnaise dressing on a slice of bread. Top with a lettuce leaf (if desired), tomato slice, and one-quarter of the tuna mixture. Top with a second slice of bread.

Nutrition facts per serving: 309 cal., 11 g total fat (2 g sat. fat), 36 mg chol., 669 mg sodium, 26 g carbo., 25 g pro.

salads

Turkey and Fruit Pasta Salad,
recipe page 146

taco SALAD

Although a tomatillo (tohm-ah-TEE-oh) looks like a small green tomato, its flavor is a combination of lemon, apple, and herbs. Look for canned tomatillos in the Mexican foods section of your supermarket.

Prep: 20 minutes
Bake: 15 minutes
Cook: 10 minutes
Makes: 6 servings

Tortilla Cups*

Tomatillo Guacamole**

8 ounces lean ground beef

3 cloves garlic, minced

1 15-ounce can dark red kidney beans, rinsed and drained

1 8-ounce jar taco sauce

¾ cup frozen whole kernel corn

1 tablespoon chili powder

8 cups torn leaf lettuce or iceberg lettuce

2 medium tomatoes, chopped

1 large green sweet pepper, chopped

¾ cup shredded sharp cheddar cheese (3 ounces)

4 green onions, thinly sliced

① Prepare Tortilla Cups, set aside. Prepare Tomatillo Guacamole; chill.

② In a medium skillet, cook ground beef and garlic until beef is brown. Drain off fat. Stir in beans, taco sauce, corn, and chili powder. Bring to boiling; reduce heat. Cover and simmer for 10 minutes.

③ In a large bowl, combine lettuce, tomatoes, green pepper, cheese, and green onions. Divide the lettuce mixture among the Tortilla Cups. Top each with some of the beef mixture and the Tomatillo Guacamole.

*Tortilla Cups: Lightly brush six 9- or 10-inch flour tortillas with a small amount of water or spray nonstick cooking spray onto one side of each tortilla. Spray nonstick cooking spray into six small oven-safe bowls or 16-ounce individual casseroles. Press tortillas, coated sides up, into bowls or casseroles. Place a ball of foil into each tortilla cup. Bake in a 350°F oven for 15 to 20 minutes or until light brown. Remove foil; cool. Remove Tortilla Cups from bowls. Serve immediately or store in an airtight container for up to 5 days.

**Tomatillo Guacamole: Rinse, drain, and finely chop 4 canned tomatillos (about ⅓ cup). In a small mixing bowl, combine tomatillos; ½ of a small seeded, peeled, and chopped avocado (about ½ cup); 2 tablespoons chopped canned green chili peppers, drained; and ⅛ teaspoon garlic salt. Cover and chill for up to 24 hours. Makes about ¾ cup.

Nutrition facts per serving: 398 cal., 17 g total fat (6 g sat. fat), 38 mg chol., 801 mg sodium, 49 g carbo., 22 g pro.

fajita BEEF SALAD

Lime does double duty in this recipe, both in the marinade and the dressing. Its tart flavor enhances the grilled beef and honey-kissed dressing.

Prep: 35 minutes
Marinate: 24 hours
Grill: 12 minutes
Makes: 4 servings

½ teaspoon finely shredded
   lime peel

⅓ cup lime juice

3 tablespoons water

4 teaspoons olive oil

¼ cup chopped onion

1 clove garlic, minced

12 ounces beef flank steak

3 tablespoons water

2 tablespoons powdered fruit
   pectin

2 tablespoons honey

6 cups torn mixed salad greens

2 small red and/or yellow
   tomatoes, cut into wedges

1 small avocado, halved,
   seeded, peeled, and
   chopped (optional)

1 In a screw-top jar, combine the lime peel, lime juice, 3 tablespoons water, and olive oil. Cover and shake well. Pour half of the lime juice mixture into a small bowl; stir in onion and garlic. Reserve remaining lime juice mixture.

2 Score the beef by making shallow diagonal cuts at 1-inch intervals in a diamond pattern. Repeat on other side. Place beef in a plastic bag set in a shallow dish. Pour the lime juice–and-onion mixture over the beef. Close bag. Marinate in the refrigerator for 24 hours, turning occasionally.

3 For dressing, in a small bowl gradually stir 3 tablespoons water into fruit pectin; stir in reserved lime juice mixture and honey. Cover and chill for 24 hours.

4 Drain beef, discarding marinade. Grill beef on the rack of an uncovered grill directly over medium coals to desired doneness, turning once. Allow 12 to 14 minutes for medium. (Or, place beef on the unheated rack of a broiler pan. Broil 3 to 4 inches from the heat to desired doneness, turning once. Allow 12 to 14 minutes for medium.)

5 To serve, thinly slice beef across grain. Arrange the greens, tomatoes, and, if desired, the avocado on four salad plates. Top with beef. Drizzle each serving with about 2 tablespoons of the dressing.

Nutrition facts per serving: 224 cal., 9 g total fat (3 g sat. fat), 40 mg chol., 72 mg sodium, 20 g carbo., 18 g pro.

pork AND MANGO SALAD

Mango chutney supplies the flavor for this exotic vinaigrette, which is a natural for complementing the flavor of pork. Look for the chutney next to the jams and jellies at the supermarket.

Start to Finish: 30 minutes
Makes: 4 servings

3 tablespoons mango chutney

2 tablespoons white wine vinegar or rice wine vinegar

1 tablespoon Dijon-style mustard or brown mustard

1 clove garlic, minced

⅛ teaspoon ground black pepper

1 tablespoon olive oil

1 tablespoon water

8 ounces pork tenderloin
Nonstick cooking spray

6 cups torn mixed salad greens

½ of an 8-ounce can sliced water chestnuts, drained

1 medium mango, peeled, seeded, and sliced, or 2 medium nectarines, sliced

2 tablespoons snipped chives

1 For vinaigrette, in a blender container or food processor bowl combine chutney, vinegar, mustard, garlic, and pepper. Cover and blend or process until smooth. In a small bowl, combine olive oil and water. With blender or food processor running, add oil mixture in a thin steady stream to chutney mixture; blend or process for 15 seconds more.

2 Trim any fat from the pork; cut into ¼-inch slices. Spray a large skillet with nonstick cooking spray. Preheat the skillet over medium-high heat. Cook pork in hot skillet for 3 to 4 minutes or until pork is no longer pink, turning once. Remove pork from skillet; keep warm.

3 In a large bowl, toss together the salad greens and water chestnuts. Pour about half of the vinaigrette over the greens mixture. Toss to coat.

4 To serve, divide greens mixture among four salad plates. Arrange some of the mango or nectarine slices and pork on the greens mixture. Drizzle each serving with about 1 tablespoon of the remaining vinaigrette. Sprinkle with the snipped chives.

Nutrition facts per serving: 192 cal., 6 g total fat (1 g sat. fat), 40 mg chol., 137 mg sodium, 21 g carbo., 14 g pro.

asian PORK-CABBAGE SALAD

Rice vinegars, known for their subtle tang and slightly sweet flavor, are used frequently in Asian cooking. Made from wine or sake, they are usually clear to pale gold in color.

Prep: 25 minutes
Chill: 4 hours
Makes: 4 servings

- 1 **3-ounce package pork-flavored ramen noodles**
- ¼ **cup rice vinegar or white wine vinegar**
- 2 **tablespoons salad oil**
- 1 **tablespoon sugar**
- ½ **teaspoon toasted sesame oil**
- ¼ **teaspoon ground black pepper**
- 1 **8.75-ounce can whole baby corn, drained**
- 1 **cup fresh pea pods or ½ of a 6-ounce package frozen pea pods, thawed**
- 2 **cups shredded cabbage**
- 8 **ounces cooked lean pork, cut into bite-size strips (1½ cups)**
- ½ **of a 14-ounce can straw mushrooms (1 cup) or one 6-ounce can whole mushrooms, drained**
- ¼ **cup sliced green onions**
- ¼ **cup sliced radishes**
  Bok choy leaves
- 2 **teaspoons sesame seeds, toasted**

1 Cook ramen noodles according to package directions, omitting the seasoning package. Drain and set aside.

2 Meanwhile, for dressing, in a screw-top jar combine the seasoning package from the ramen noodles, the vinegar, salad oil, sugar, sesame oil, and pepper. Cover and shake well to dissolve seasonings.

3 Cut each ear of baby corn in half crosswise. If using fresh pea pods, trim ends and remove strings. In a large bowl, combine cooked noodles, baby corn, pea pods, cabbage, pork, mushrooms, green onions, and radishes. Shake dressing well. Pour over cabbage mixture; toss gently to coat. Cover and chill for 4 to 24 hours.

4 Line dinner plates with bok choy leaves. Divide pork mixture among plates. Sprinkle each salad with sesame seeds.

Nutrition facts per serving: 386 cal., 20 g total fat (4 g sat. fat), 52 mg chol., 830 mg sodium, 31 g carbo., 23 g pro.

turkey AND FRUIT PASTA SALAD

For a slightly smoky flavor, use the turkey ham option. For additional variety and color, use fresh blueberries or raspberries in place of the strawberries.

Prep: 25 minutes
Chill: 4 hours
Makes: 4 servings

- **1 cup dried gemelli or 1⅓ cups dried rotini**
- **1½ cups chopped cooked turkey, chicken, or turkey ham (about 8 ounces)**
- **2 green onions, sliced**
- **⅓ cup lime or lemon juice**
- **¼ cup salad oil**
- **1 tablespoon honey**
- **2 teaspoons snipped fresh thyme or ½ teaspoon dried thyme, crushed**
- **2 medium nectarines or large plums, sliced**
- **1 cup halved strawberries**

1. Cook pasta according to package directions; drain. Rinse with cold water; drain again.

2. In a large bowl, combine cooked pasta, turkey, and green onions; toss gently to combine.

3. For dressing, in a screw-top jar combine lime juice, oil, honey, and thyme. Cover and shake well. Pour dressing over pasta mixture; toss gently to coat. Cover and chill for 4 to 24 hours.

4. Just before serving, add the nectarines and strawberries; toss gently to combine.

Nutrition facts per serving: 382 cal., 17 g total fat (3 g sat. fat), 40 mg chol., 40 mg sodium, 37 g carbo., 20 g pro.

mango SALAD WITH TURKEY

To save time, prepare the lime vinaigrette ahead and cover and chill for up to 4 hours. Shake the dressing before drizzling over the salad. For an extra burst of citrus flavor, serve the salad with lime wedges.

Start to Finish: 30 minutes
Makes: 4 servings

¼ **cup salad oil**

¼ **teaspoon finely shredded lime peel**

2 **tablespoons lime juice**

¼ **teaspoon grated fresh ginger**

6 **cups torn mixed greens**

4 **mangoes, seeded, peeled, and cut into thin slices**

8 **ounces cooked smoked turkey or chicken, cut into thin, bite-size strips**

1 **green onion, thinly sliced**

¼ **cup snipped fresh cilantro**
  Lime wedges (optional)

1 In a screw-top jar, combine salad oil, lime peel, lime juice, and ginger. Cover and shake well. Divide greens among four salad plates. Arrange one-quarter of the mango, smoked turkey, and green onion on each plate of greens. Sprinkle with cilantro. Drizzle vinaigrette over salad. If desired, serve with lime wedges on the side.

Nutrition facts per serving: 321 cal., 15 g total fat (2 g sat. fat), 25 mg chol., 417 mg sodium, 39 g carbo., 12 g pro.

chicken SALAD WITH RASPBERRY VINAIGRETTE

If you like, arrange all the ingredients on a large glass salad plate and pass the dressing in a small cruet.

Prep: 20 minutes
Grill: 12 minutes
Chill: up to 2 hours
Makes: 4 servings

- 2 cups torn leaf lettuce
- 2 cups torn radicchio
- 2 cups torn arugula
- 1 medium Belgian endive, cut up
- 1 tablespoon Dijon-style mustard
- 1 tablespoon honey
- ¼ teaspoon salt
- ⅛ teaspoon ground black pepper
- 4 medium skinless, boneless chicken breast halves (about 1 pound total)
- 2 medium oranges, peeled and sliced
- 1 pink grapefruit, peeled and sectioned
- 1 avocado, halved, seeded, peeled, and sliced
- 2 green onions, thinly bias-sliced
  Raspberry Vinaigrette*
  Fresh red raspberries (optional)

1 In a large bowl, combine the leaf lettuce, radicchio, arugula, and Belgian endive; toss gently to mix. Cover and chill for up to 2 hours. For sauce, in a small bowl combine the Dijon mustard, honey, salt, and pepper; set aside.

2 Place chicken on the rack of an uncovered grill directly over medium coals. Grill for 12 to 15 minutes or until no longer pink (170°F), turning once and brushing with sauce in the last 2 minutes of grilling. Cool chicken slightly; cut into thin strips.

3 Arrange the lettuce mixture on dinner plates. Arrange chicken strips, oranges, grapefruit sections, avocado slices, and green onions on lettuce mixture. Drizzle some of the Raspberry Vinaigrette over salads. If desired, garnish with fresh raspberries.

*Raspberry Vinaigrette: In a blender container, combine one 10-ounce package frozen red raspberries, thawed; 2 tablespoons olive oil or salad oil; 2 tablespoons lemon juice; and 1 clove garlic, minced. Cover and blend until smooth. Press the berry mixture through a fine-mesh sieve; discard seeds. Cover and chill until serving time. Reserve any remaining dressing for another use.

Nutrition facts per serving: 331 cal., 15 g total fat (1 g sat. fat), 59 mg chol., 295 mg sodium, 26 g carbo., 25 g pro.

COUSCOUS CHICKEN SALAD

Handy refrigerated lemon-pepper or Italian-style chicken breast strips save you the work and time of cutting up, seasoning, and cooking your own chicken.

Start to Finish: 15 minutes
Makes: 4 servings

1 **14-ounce can chicken broth**

1¼ **cups quick-cooking couscous**

½ **cup mango chutney, large pieces cut up**

¼ **cup bottled olive oil and vinegar salad dressing, white wine vinaigrette salad dressing, or roasted garlic vinaigrette salad dressing**

1 **6-ounce package cooked, refrigerated lemon-pepper or Italian-style chicken breast strips, cut into bite-size pieces (about 1½ cups)**

½ **cup golden raisins or raisins (optional)**

1 **cup coarsely chopped radishes or seeded cucumber**

Salt

Ground black pepper

1 **small cucumber, cut into spears**

1 In a medium saucepan, bring chicken broth to boiling. Stir in couscous. Cover and remove from heat. Let stand for 5 minutes. Fluff couscous lightly with a fork.

2 In a medium bowl, combine mango chutney and salad dressing. Add chicken, raisins (if desired), chopped radishes, and cooked couscous. Toss to coat. Season to taste with salt and pepper. Serve with cucumber spears.

Nutrition facts per serving: 411 cal., 10 g total fat (2 g sat. fat), 22 mg chol., 848 mg sodium, 63 g carbo., 16 g pro.

szechwan CHICKEN SALAD

Jicama, a crisp root vegetable, stars in this grilled chicken salad with carrot, cucumbers, and enoki mushrooms. A light sprinkling of peanuts adds crunch and flavor.

Prep: 25 minutes
Marinate: 4 to 24 hours
Grill: 12 minutes
Makes: 4 servings

- 2 **teaspoons cooking oil**
- 1 **teaspoon toasted sesame oil**
- 3 **cloves garlic, minced**
- 2 **tablespoons grated fresh ginger**
- ⅓ **cup rice vinegar or white wine vinegar**
- 2 **tablespoons reduced-sodium soy sauce**
- 4 **skinless, boneless chicken breast halves (12 ounces total)**
- 1 **fresh jalapeño pepper, seeded and chopped**
- ½ **teaspoon sugar**
- 1 **medium carrot, cut into matchstick strips**
- 1 **cup peeled jicama cut in matchstick strips**
- 4 **lettuce leaves**
- 2 **medium cucumbers, quartered lengthwise and cut into ¼-inch slices**
- 1⅓ **cups enoki mushrooms**
- 2 **green onions, sliced**
- 2 **tablespoons chopped unsalted cocktail peanuts**

1 In a small saucepan, heat cooking oil and sesame oil over medium-high heat for 1 minute. Cook and stir garlic and ginger in hot oil for 15 seconds. Remove saucepan from heat; stir in vinegar, soy sauce, and 3 tablespoons water. Cool completely.

2 Rinse chicken; pat dry. Place in a plastic bag set in a shallow dish. Pour half of the soy mixture over the chicken; reserve remaining soy mixture. Close bag. Marinate in the refrigerator for 4 to 24 hours.

3 Meanwhile, for dressing, in a small bowl stir together reserved soy mixture, 2 tablespoons water, the jalapeño pepper, and sugar. Cover and chill for 4 to 24 hours.

4 Drain chicken, discarding marinade. Grill chicken on the lightly greased rack of an uncovered grill directly over medium coals for 12 to 15 minutes or until chicken is tender and no longer pink, turning once. Cut chicken into bite-size strips. Combine the carrot and jicama. To serve, line four salad plates with the lettuce. Top with carrot mixture, cucumbers, chicken, mushrooms, green onions, and peanuts. Stir dressing; drizzle 1 tablespoon dressing over each serving.

Nutrition facts per serving: 200 cal., 7 g total fat (1 g sat. fat), 45 mg chol., 231 mg sodium, 15 g carbo., 20 g pro.

curried CHICKEN SALAD

Curry powder, used in small doses, really perks up a recipe like this one. The celery and apples lend crunch, while the wild rice adds a satisfying chewiness to this delicious salad.

Prep: 30 minutes
Chill: 1 to 4 hours
Makes: about 6 (1-cup) servings

12 **ounces skinless, boneless chicken breast halves**

1 **cup water**

¼ **teaspoon salt**

⅔ **cup light or fat-free mayonnaise dressing or salad dressing**

¼ **cup fat-free milk**

2 **teaspoons curry powder**

¼ **teaspoon salt**

2 **cups chopped red apples**

2 **cups cooked wild rice, chilled**

1½ **cups sliced celery**

½ **cup golden raisins**

Romaine or spinach leaves (optional)

1 In a medium skillet, combine the chicken, water, and ¼ teaspoon salt. Bring to boiling; reduce heat. Simmer, covered, for 12 to 14 minutes or until the chicken is tender and no longer pink. Drain well; let cool. Cut the chicken into bite-size pieces.

2 Meanwhile, for the dressing, in a small bowl stir together the mayonnaise dressing or salad dressing, milk, curry powder, and ¼ teaspoon salt.

3 In a large bowl, stir together cooked chicken, apples, cooked wild rice, celery, and raisins; stir in the dressing. Cover and chill for 1 to 4 hours. If desired, serve on romaine or spinach leaves.

Nutrition facts per serving: 281 cal., 11 g total fat (2 g sat. fat), 30 mg chol., 436 mg sodium, 33 g carbo., 14 g pro.

ginger-lime CHICKEN SALAD

Yogurt serves as a healthy alternative to mayonnaise in this tangy, quick-to-prepare chicken salad.

Prep: 10 minutes
Chill: 30 minutes
Makes: 4 servings

¼ **cup fat-free plain yogurt**

2 **tablespoons lime juice**

2 **teaspoons grated fresh ginger**

2 **cups chopped cooked chicken breast**

1 **cup snow pea pods, bias-cut lengthwise**

1 **cup thinly sliced celery**

1 **tablespoon thinly sliced red onion**

1 In a medium bowl, combine yogurt, lime juice, and ginger. Add chicken, stirring to coat. Cover and chill for at least 30 minutes. In a medium bowl, toss together pea pods, celery, and onion. Place the vegetable mixture in four salad bowls. Top with the chicken mixture.

Nutrition facts per serving: 147 cal., 3 g total fat (1 g sat. fat), 60 mg chol., 86 mg sodium, 5 g carbo., 23 g pro.

fruit AND CHICKEN SALAD

Frozen juice concentrates are ideal ingredients for making low-fat dressings. Because concentrates deliver a lot of punch in a small amount, you don't need to use much. Here, concentrate also lends body to the dressing.

Prep: 25 minutes
Chill: 2 to 4 hours
Makes: 4 servings

½ **cup fat-free dairy sour cream**

½ **cup fat-free mayonnaise dressing or salad dressing**

1 **tablespoon frozen orange juice concentrate, thawed**

⅛ **teaspoon ground ginger**
  Pinch crushed red pepper

3 **green onions, sliced (⅓ cup)**

2 **cups thinly sliced celery**

1½ **cups seedless red or green grapes, halved**

1½ **cups chopped cooked chicken**

½ **cup dried apricots, cut into slivers**

4 **lettuce leaves**

2 **plum tomatoes, thinly sliced**

1 **cucumber, thinly sliced**

1 For dressing, stir together the sour cream, mayonnaise dressing or salad dressing, orange juice concentrate, ginger, and red pepper. Stir in green onions.

2 In a large bowl, toss together celery, grapes, chicken, and apricots; stir in the dressing. Cover and chill for 2 to 4 hours.

3 To serve, line four salad plates with lettuce leaves. Arrange tomatoes and cucumber on top of lettuce. Top with chicken mixture.

Nutrition facts per serving: 264 cal., 3 g total fat (1 g sat. fat), 44 mg chol., 511 mg sodium, 40 g carbo., 21 g pro.

asian PEA POD SALAD

Start to Finish: 20 minutes
Makes: 6 servings

6 cups torn romaine lettuce

2 cups fresh pea pods, trimmed
and halved lengthwise

⅓ cup bottled Italian salad
dressing

1 tablespoon hoisin sauce

1 tablespoon sesame seeds,
toasted

4 radishes, coarsely shredded

1 In a large salad bowl, toss together the lettuce and pea pods. In a small bowl, stir together the dressing and hoisin sauce. Pour over lettuce mixture and toss to coat. Sprinkle with sesame seeds and radishes.

Nutrition facts per serving: 98 cal., 7 g total fat (1 g sat. fat), 0 mg chol., 153 mg sodium, 6 g carbo., 2 g pro.

grilled VEGETABLE SALAD WITH GARLIC DRESSING

Vegetables, sweet and smoky from the grill, give pasta and cheese a jolt of flavor and color. By doing the grilling ahead and storing the savory dressing in the refrigerator, this maximum-impact dish is done in the time it takes to simmer pasta.

Start to Finish: 30 minutes
Makes: 4 servings

- 2 **red and/or yellow sweet peppers**
- 2 **Japanese eggplants, halved lengthwise**
- 2 **medium zucchini or yellow summer squash, halved lengthwise, or 8 to 10 yellow sunburst or pattypan squash****
- 1 **tablespoon olive oil**
- 2 **cups packaged dried rigatoni or mostaccioli**
  Roasted Garlic Dressing*
- ¾ **cup cubed fontina cheese (3 ounces)**
- 1 **to 2 tablespoons snipped fresh parsley**
  Fresh parsley sprigs (optional)

1 Halve sweet peppers lengthwise; remove and discard stems, seeds, and membranes. Brush sweet peppers, eggplants, and squash with olive oil.

2 Grill vegetables on an uncovered grill directly over medium-hot coals for 8 to 12 minutes or until the vegetables are tender, turning occasionally. Remove vegetables from grill; cool slightly. Cut vegetables into 1-inch pieces.

3 Meanwhile, cook the pasta according to package directions. Drain pasta; rinse with cold water. Drain again. In a large bowl, combine the pasta and grilled vegetables. Pour Roasted Garlic Dressing over pasta mixture. Toss gently to coat. Stir in fontina cheese. Sprinkle with snipped parsley. If desired, garnish with parsley sprigs.

*Roasted Garlic Dressing: In a screw-top jar combine 3 tablespoons balsamic vinegar or red wine vinegar, 2 tablespoons olive oil, 1 tablespoon water, 1 teaspoon bottled roasted minced garlic, ¼ teaspoon salt, and ¼ teaspoon black pepper. Cover and shake well.

**Note: If using sunburst or pattypan squash, cook the squash in a small amount of boiling water for 3 minutes before grilling.

Nutrition facts per serving: 369 cal., 19 g total fat (6 g sat. fat), 61 mg chol., 317 mg sodium, 40 g carbo., 12 g pro.

spinach PASTA SALAD

The basil, prosciutto, and pine nuts—classic Italian favorites—keep this cool pasta salad packed with interesting flavors.

Prep: 25 minutes
Chill: 4 hours
Makes: 6 servings

- **8 ounces dried ziti or other medium pasta**
- **1 cup lightly packed spinach leaves**
- **¼ cup lightly packed basil leaves**
- **2 cloves garlic, quartered**
- **2 tablespoons finely shredded Parmesan cheese**
- **⅛ teaspoon salt**
- **⅛ teaspoon ground black pepper**
- **1 tablespoon olive oil**
- **1 tablespoon water**
- **½ cup fat-free or light mayonnaise dressing or salad dressing**
- **6 spinach leaves**
- **6 radicchio leaves (optional)**
- **1 ounce chopped prosciutto or ham**
- **2 tablespoons pine nuts, toasted**

1 Cook pasta according to package directions; drain. Rinse with cold water; drain again. Set aside.

2 Meanwhile, in a blender container or food processor bowl combine the 1 cup spinach, the basil, garlic, cheese, salt, and pepper. Add oil and water; cover and blend or process until nearly smooth and mixture forms a paste, scraping down sides of container frequently. Combine mayonnaise dressing and spinach mixture. Add to pasta and toss until well coated. Cover and chill for 4 to 24 hours.

3 To serve, line a salad bowl with spinach leaves and, if desired, radicchio leaves. Spoon salad into lined bowl. Sprinkle with chopped prosciutto and pine nuts.

Nutrition facts per serving: 304 cal., 15 g total fat (4 g sat. fat), 18 mg chol., 494 mg sodium, 32 g carbo., 12 g pro.

shrimp SALAD

This salad has the makings of an elegant meal and deserves to be included on a special celebration menu. The flavors of asparagus and shrimp flourish with the addition of a balsamic vinaigrette.

Prep: 25 minutes
Chill: 4 to 24 hours
Makes: 4 servings

2 tablespoons dried tomato pieces (not oil-packed)
¼ cup balsamic vinegar
2 tablespoons olive oil
1 tablespoon snipped fresh basil
2 teaspoons Dijon-style mustard
2 cloves garlic, minced
¼ teaspoon sugar
⅛ teaspoon ground black pepper
12 ounces fresh or frozen peeled shrimp
4 cups water
1 clove garlic
8 ounces asparagus, cut into 2-inch lengths
6 cups torn mixed salad greens
2 medium pears, thinly sliced

1 In a small bowl, pour boiling water over tomato pieces to cover; let stand for 2 minutes. Drain.

2 For dressing, in a screw-top jar combine tomato pieces, vinegar, olive oil, basil, mustard, minced garlic, sugar, and pepper. Cover and shake well. If desired, cover and chill for up to 24 hours.

3 Thaw shrimp, if frozen. In a large saucepan, bring the water and the 1 clove garlic to boiling; add asparagus. Return to boiling. Simmer, uncovered, for 4 minutes. Add shrimp. Return to boiling. Simmer, uncovered, for 1 to 3 minutes more or until shrimp are opaque. Drain, discarding garlic. Rinse under cold running water; drain well. Cover and chill for 4 to 24 hours.

4 To serve, divide greens and pears among four salad plates. Top each with some of the shrimp and asparagus. Shake dressing; drizzle each serving with about 2 tablespoons of the dressing.

Nutrition facts per serving: 221 cal., 8 g total fat (1 g sat. fat), 131 mg chol., 260 mg sodium, 21 g carbo., 17 g pro.

spinach-pasta SALAD WITH SHRIMP

If you prefer, make the pasta-and-shrimp mixture up to 24 hours ahead and chill it. Then toss it with the spinach and goat cheese just before serving.

Start to Finish: 25 minutes
Makes: 6 servings

1 **cup dried elbow macaroni or tiny shell pasta**

1 **pound frozen cooked shrimp, thawed, or 1 pound cooked peeled and deveined shrimp (from supermarket deli)**

1 **cup chopped red sweet pepper (from supermarket salad bar)**

⅓ **cup bottled creamy onion or Caesar salad dressing**

2 **tablespoons snipped fresh dill (optional)**

Salt

Freshly ground black pepper

1 **6-ounce package baby spinach**

4 **ounces goat cheese (chèvre), sliced, or feta cheese, crumbled**

1. Cook macaroni according to package directions. Drain well. Rinse with cold water; drain again.

2. In an extra-large bowl, combine the cooked macaroni, shrimp, and sweet pepper. Drizzle with salad dressing. If desired, sprinkle with dill. Toss to coat. Season to taste with salt and black pepper.

3. Divide spinach among six salad plates or bowls. Top with shrimp mixture and cheese.

Nutrition facts per serving: 247 cal., 10 g total fat (4 g sat. fat), 156 mg chol., 435 mg sodium, 17 g carbo., 23 g pro.

salmon SALAD

This salad will remind you of a Caesar salad—without the raw eggs, anchovies, high fat, and calories. Plain yogurt adds the creamy texture to the garlic and lemon dressing.

Prep: 20 minutes
Chill: 30 minutes
Broil: 8 to 12 minutes
Makes: 4 servings

- 2 **tablespoons olive oil**
- 5 **cloves garlic, thinly sliced**
- 2 **tablespoons lemon juice**
- 1 **tablespoon Worcestershire sauce**
- 1 **tablespoon Dijon-style mustard**
- 1 **tablespoon water**
- ½ **teaspoon ground black pepper**
- ⅓ **cup fat-free plain yogurt**
- 12 **ounces fresh or frozen skinless, boneless salmon fillets, 1 inch thick**
- **Nonstick cooking spray**
- 10 **cups torn romaine**
- ½ **cup thinly sliced red onion**
- ¼ **cup freshly grated Parmesan cheese**
- 1 **cup cherry tomatoes, halved**
- ½ **cup pitted ripe olives, halved (optional)**

1 In a small saucepan, heat olive oil over medium-low heat. Cook and stir garlic in hot oil for 1 to 2 minutes or until garlic is lightly golden. Transfer garlic to a blender container. Add lemon juice, Worcestershire sauce, mustard, water, and pepper. Cover; blend until combined. Reserve 2 tablespoons of garlic mixture; set aside. Add yogurt to remaining garlic mixture in blender. Cover and blend until smooth. Chill until serving time.

2 Thaw salmon, if frozen. Rinse salmon; pat dry. Brush the reserved garlic mixture evenly over salmon. Cover and chill for 30 minutes.

3 Spray the unheated rack of a broiler pan with nonstick cooking spray. Place the salmon on the rack. Broil 4 to 5 inches from heat for 8 to 12 minutes or until salmon flakes easily when tested with a fork, turning once.

4 Meanwhile, in a large bowl toss romaine, onion, and Parmesan cheese with the chilled yogurt mixture. Divide romaine mixture among four salad plates. Place one salmon fillet on each salad. Top with tomatoes and, if desired, olives.

Nutrition facts per serving: 234 cal., 13 g total fat (3 g sat. fat), 21 mg chol., 331 mg sodium, 12 g carbo., 19 g pro.

simple SIDE DISHES

Green Bean Salad, *recipe page 190*

lemony MIXED VEGETABLES

Be creative with seasonings! The inspired combination of coriander, oregano, and lemon peel adds character to this simple vegetable side dish.

Prep: 20 minutes
Cook: 18 minutes
Makes: 6 (¾-cup) servings

- 1 **cup reduced-sodium chicken broth**
- ¼ **teaspoon ground coriander**
- ⅛ **teaspoon salt**
- ⅛ **teaspoon ground black pepper**
- 8 **ounces green beans, cut into 2-inch lengths (about 2 cups)**
- 2 **cups thinly bias-sliced carrots**
- 1 **cup cauliflower florets**
- ½ **of a medium red sweet pepper, cut into 1-inch pieces**
- 1 **tablespoon snipped fresh oregano or 1 teaspoon dried oregano, crushed**
- 1 **tablespoon cold water**
- 1½ **teaspoons cornstarch**
- ½ **teaspoon finely shredded lemon peel**
- 4 **teaspoons lemon juice**

1 In a large saucepan, combine the chicken broth, coriander, salt, and black pepper. Bring to boiling; add green beans. Return to boiling; reduce heat. Simmer, covered, for 10 minutes. Add carrots, cauliflower, and sweet pepper. Return to boiling; reduce heat. Simmer, covered, for 4 to 5 minutes more or until vegetables are crisp-tender.

2 Using a slotted spoon, transfer vegetables to a serving bowl, reserving broth mixture in saucepan. Cover vegetables; keep warm.

3 In a small bowl, stir together oregano, water, cornstarch, and lemon peel; stir into broth mixture in saucepan. Cook and stir over medium heat until slightly thickened and bubbly. Cook and stir for 2 minutes more. Stir in lemon juice. Pour thickened broth mixture over vegetables. Toss lightly to coat.

Nutrition facts per serving: 49 cal., 0 g total fat (0 g sat. fat), 0 mg chol., 184 mg sodium, 11 g carbo., 2 g pro.

vegetable PRIMAVERA

The Italian word primavera *refers to the use of fresh vegetables, and that is what this recipe features. Squash, carrots, red pepper, and broccoli combine to create a festival of colors.*

Start to Finish: 20 minutes
Makes: 6 (¾-cup) servings

- 3 **tablespoons reduced-sodium chicken broth**
- 1 **tablespoon Dijon-style mustard**
- 1 **tablespoon olive oil**
- 2 **teaspoons white wine vinegar**
  Nonstick cooking spray
- 1½ **cups sliced yellow summer squash**
- 1 **cup packaged peeled baby carrots**
- 1 **cup chopped red sweet pepper**
- 3 **cups broccoli florets**
- 2 **tablespoons snipped fresh parsley**

1 In a small bowl, combine 1 tablespoon of the chicken broth, the mustard, olive oil, and vinegar. Set aside.

2 Spray a large nonstick skillet with nonstick cooking spray. Preheat the skillet over medium heat. Cook and stir squash, carrots, and sweet pepper in hot skillet for about 5 minutes or until nearly tender. Add broccoli and remaining chicken broth to skillet. Cook, covered, for about 3 minutes or until broccoli is crisp-tender.

3 Stir in the mustard mixture; heat through. To serve, sprinkle with parsley.

Nutrition facts per serving: 56 cal., 3 g total fat (0 g sat. fat), 0 mg chol., 114 mg sodium, 7 g carbo., 2 g pro.

Spray for Success

Nonstick cooking spray not only eliminates the mess of greasing pans, it also saves on fat and calories. For added pizzazz, look for roasted garlic-, olive oil-, and butter-flavored sprays. Compare the difference of using nonstick spray in place of oil, margarine, or butter:

- Nonstick cooking spray (1-second spray) <1 g fat 7 calories
- Butter/margarine (1 teaspoon) 4 g fat 35 calories
- Oil (1 teaspoon) 5 g fat 41 calories

roasted ASPARAGUS

Prep: 10 minutes
Roast: 15 minutes
Oven: 450°F
Makes: 8 servings

2 **pounds fresh asparagus, trimmed**

2 **tablespoons olive oil**

¼ **cup grated Parmesan cheese**

¼ **cup butter, softened**

¼ **cup finely chopped radishes**

2 **tablespoon snipped fresh chives**

1 **tablespoon lemon juice**

1 Preheat oven to 450°F. Place asparagus in a 3-quart rectangular baking dish. Drizzle with oil and sprinkle with cheese. Roast, uncovered, for about 15 minutes or until crisp-tender, using tongs to lightly toss twice during roasting.

2 Meanwhile, in a small bowl, combine butter, radishes, chives, and lemon juice. Transfer asparagus to a warm platter. Serve with butter mixture.

Nutrition facts per serving: 105 cal., 10 g total fat (5 g sat. fat), 17 mg chol., 82 mg sodium, 3 g carbo., 2 g pro.

great GREEK GREEN BEANS

Prep: 10 minutes
Cook: 20 minutes
Makes: 6 servings

½ **cup chopped onion**

1 **clove garlic, minced**

2 **tablespoons olive oil**

1 **28-ounce can diced tomatoes, undrained**

¼ **cup sliced pitted ripe olives**

1 **teaspoon dried oregano, crushed**

2 **9-ounce packages or one 16-ounce package frozen French-cut green beans, thawed and drained**

½ **cup crumbled feta cheese (2 ounces)**

1 In a large skillet, cook onion and garlic in hot oil for about 5 minutes or until tender. Add undrained tomatoes, olives, and oregano. Bring to boiling; reduce heat. Boil gently, uncovered, for 10 minutes. Add beans. Return to boiling. Boil gently, uncovered, for about 8 minutes or to desired consistency and beans are tender.

2 Transfer to a serving bowl; sprinkle with cheese. If desired, serve with a slotted spoon.

Nutrition facts per serving: 132 cal., 7 g total fat (2 g sat. fat), 8 mg chol., 419 mg sodium, 15 g carbo., 4 g pro.

caramelized BRUSSELS SPROUTS

Prep: 15 minutes
Cook: 21 minutes
Makes: 8 servings

5 cups small, firm, fresh
  Brussels sprouts (about
  1½ pounds)
¼ cup sugar
2 tablespoons butter
¼ cup red wine vinegar
⅓ cup water
½ teaspoon salt

1. Prepare the Brussels sprouts by peeling off two or three of the dark outer leaves from each Brussels sprout; trim stem ends.

2. In a large skillet, heat sugar over medium-high heat until it begins to melt, shaking pan occasionally to heat sugar evenly. Once sugar starts to melt, reduce heat and cook until sugar begins to turn brown. Add butter; stir until melted. Add vinegar. Cook and stir for 1 minute.

3. Carefully add the water and salt. Bring to boiling; add Brussels sprouts. Return to boiling; reduce heat. Simmer, covered, for 6 minutes.

4. Uncover and cook for about 15 minutes more or until most of the liquid has been absorbed and the sprouts are coated with a golden glaze, gently stirring occasionally.

Nutrition facts per serving: 76 cal., 3 g total fat (2 g sat. fat), 8 mg chol., 155 mg sodium, 11 g carbo., 2 g pro.

dino KALE SAUTÉ

If you enjoy kale in salads, you'll love this wilted greens side dish that's sprinkled with toasted bread crumbs, Worcestershire sauce, and a squeeze of lemon.

Start to Finish: 15 minutes
Makes: 4 servings

12 ounces dinosaur kale or regular kale, cut or torn into 1- to 2-inch pieces (about 12 cups)

2 tablespoons olive oil

¼ cup soft sourdough or French loaf bread crumbs

⅛ teaspoon ground black pepper

1 teaspoon Worcestershire sauce for chicken

Lemon wedges (optional)

1 Rinse kale leaves thoroughly under cold running water. Drain well; set aside.

2 In a small skillet, heat 2 teaspoons of the oil over medium heat. Add bread crumbs; cook and stir for 1 to 2 minutes or until browned. Season with pepper; set aside.

3 In a large nonstick skillet, heat the remaining 4 teaspoons oil. Add kale; cover and cook for 1 minute. Uncover and cook and stir for about 1 minute more or just until wilted.

4 Transfer kale to a serving dish. Drizzle with Worcestershire sauce. Sprinkle with the browned bread crumbs. If desired, squeeze lemon over all.

Nutrition facts per serving: 89 cal., 5 g total fat (1 g sat. fat), 0 mg chol., 53 mg sodium, 9 g carbo., 2 g pro.

cauliflower WITH LEMON DRESSING

Serrano ham and manchego cheese are a seasoned ham and a sheep's-milk cheese imported from Spain. Look for them at specialty food shops.

Start to Finish: 20 minutes
Makes: 4 servings

- 2 **small heads cauliflower**
- ½ **cup water**
- 2 **to 3 ounces thinly sliced Serrano ham, prosciutto, or cooked ham**
- 1 **ounce manchego cheese or Monterey Jack cheese, thinly shaved**
- ¼ **cup olive oil or cooking oil**
- 2 **tablespoons lemon juice**
- ½ **teaspoon salt**
- ½ **teaspoon bottled minced garlic**
- ¼ **teaspoon sugar**
- ¼ **teaspoon dry mustard**
- ¼ **teaspoon ground black pepper**
- 2 **tablespoons pine nuts, toasted**
- 2 **tablespoons capers, drained**

1 Remove heavy leaves and tough stems from cauliflower; cut cauliflower into wedges. Place cauliflower wedges in a microwave-safe 3-quart casserole. Add the water. Microwave, covered, on 100% power (high) for 7 to 9 minutes or just until tender. Remove with a slotted spoon to serving plates. Top with ham and cheese.

2 Meanwhile, in a screw-top jar, combine oil, lemon juice, salt, garlic, sugar, mustard, and pepper. Cover and shake well to combine; drizzle over cauliflower. Sprinkle with pine nuts and capers.

Nutrition facts per serving: 207 cal., 18 g total fat (3 g sat. fat), 10 mg chol., 848 mg sodium, 7 g carbo., 9 g pro.

barbecued LIMAS

A spunky barbecue sauce that starts with canned soup makes this old-fashioned bean-and-bacon combination a tasty reason to get out the can opener.

Start to Finish: 25 minutes
Makes: 6 servings

- 1 **16-ounce package frozen baby lima beans**
- 4 **slices bacon, cut into ½-inch pieces**
- ½ **cup chopped onion**
- 1 **teaspoon bottled minced garlic**
- 1 **10.75-ounce can condensed tomato soup**
- 2 **tablespoons packed brown sugar**
- 1 **tablespoon white vinegar**
- 1 **tablespoon Worcestershire sauce**
- 2 **teaspoons yellow mustard**
- 1 **teaspoon chili powder**

1 In a large saucepan, cook lima beans according to package directions; drain and set aside.

2 Meanwhile, in another large saucepan, cook bacon, onion, and garlic over medium heat until bacon is brown and onion is tender. Stir in tomato soup, brown sugar, vinegar, Worcestershire sauce, mustard, and chili powder. Bring to boiling; reduce heat. Cover and simmer for 5 minutes.

3 Stir cooked lima beans into tomato soup mixture; heat through.

Nutrition facts per serving: 195 cal., 3 g total fat (1 g sat. fat), 5 mg chol., 487 mg sodium, 34 g carbo., 9 g pro.

chipotle COLESLAW

Chipotle peppers are simply smoked jalapeño peppers. This recipe calls for ground chipotle chile pepper, which gives the coleslaw a spicy kick.

Start to Finish: 20 minutes
Makes: 6 servings

⅓ cup fat-free mayonnaise

1 tablespoon lime juice

2 teaspoons honey

¼ teaspoon ground cumin

⅛ to ¼ teaspoon ground chipotle chile pepper

3 cups shredded green cabbage

¾ cup whole kernel corn, thawed if frozen

¾ cup chopped red sweet pepper

⅓ cup thinly sliced red onion

⅓ cup chopped fresh cilantro

1 In a small bowl, stir together mayonnaise, lime juice, honey, cumin, and chipotle chile pepper.

2 In a large bowl, combine cabbage, corn, sweet pepper, onion, and cilantro. Pour mayonnaise mixture over cabbage mixture. Toss lightly to coat. Serve immediately or cover and chill for up to 24 hours.

Nutrition facts per serving: 55 cal., 0.7 g total fat (0 g sat. fat), 1.3 mg chol., 122 mg sodium, 13 g carbo., 2 g pro.

black BEAN SLAW WITH SOY-GINGER DRESSING

Prep: 15 minutes
Chill: 4 hours
Makes: 4 servings

- ½ of a 15-ounce can black beans, rinsed and drained
- 3 cups purchased coleslaw mix
- 1 medium green apple, cored and chopped (⅔ cup)
- ½ cup chopped red sweet pepper
- 2 tablespoons cider vinegar
- 1 tablespoon reduced-sodium soy sauce
- 1 tablespoon peanut oil
- 1 teaspoon grated fresh ginger
- 1 teaspoon honey
- ⅛ teaspoon ground black pepper

1 In a large bowl, combine black beans, coleslaw mix, apple, and sweet pepper. In a small screw-top jar, combine vinegar, soy sauce, peanut oil, ginger, honey, and black pepper; cover and shake well. Pour over cabbage mixture; toss to mix. Cover and chill for 4 hours or overnight.

Nutrition facts per serving: 217 cal., 7 g total fat (1 g sat. fat), 0 mg chol., 577 mg sodium, 36 g carbo., 9 g pro.

really RED COLESLAW

Take a break from ordinary slaw with this impressively red fruity delight.

Start to Finish: 15 minutes
Makes: 8 servings

1   **10-ounce package shredded red cabbage (about 6 cups)**

1   **medium red onion, slivered (1 cup)**

½   **cup dried tart red cherries**

½   **cup bottled raspberry vinaigrette salad dressing**

1   **tablespoon seedless red raspberry preserves**

1   In a large bowl, combine red cabbage, red onion, and dried cherries; set aside. In a small bowl, stir together vinaigrette and preserves; pour over cabbage mixture. Toss gently to coat.

Make Ahead: Prepare as directed. Cover and chill for up to 6 hours.

Nutrition facts per serving: 108 cal., 6 g total fat (1 g sat. fat), 0 mg chol., 5 mg sodium, 12 g carbo., 1 g pro.

greek SALAD

Start to Finish: 15 minutes
Makes: 4 servings

6 cups packaged torn romaine
and iceberg lettuce blend

¼ cup thin red onion wedges

¼ cup red sweet pepper strips

¼ cup crumbled feta cheese

2 tablespoons pitted ripe black
olives, halved

½ cup bottled red wine
vinaigrette

1 In a large bowl, toss together lettuce blend, onion, sweet pepper, feta, and olives. Drizzle with vinaigrette; toss to coat.

Nutrition facts per serving: 183 cal., 17 g total fat (3 g sat. fat), 8 mg chol., 728 mg sodium, 6 g carbo., 2 g pro.

greek VEGETABLE SALAD

Start to Finish: 30 minutes
Makes: 8 servings

- 2 **cups chopped tomatoes**
- 1 **cup chopped cucumber**
- ½ **cup chopped yellow, red, and/or green sweet pepper**
- ¼ **cup chopped red onion**
- 1½ **teaspoons snipped fresh thyme or ½ teaspoon dried thyme, crushed**
- 1 **teaspoon snipped fresh oregano or ¼ teaspoon dried oregano, crushed**
- 2 **tablespoons white balsamic vinegar or regular balsamic vinegar**
- 2 **tablespoons olive oil**
- **Leaf lettuce (optional)**
- ½ **cup crumbled feta cheese**

1 In a large bowl, combine tomatoes, cucumber, sweet pepper, red onion, thyme, and oregano. For dressing, in a small bowl, whisk together vinegar and olive oil. Pour dressing over vegetable mixture. Toss gently to coat.

2 If desired, line a serving bowl with lettuce; spoon in vegetable mixture. Sprinkle with feta cheese.

Nutrition facts per serving: 65 cal., 5 g total fat (1 g sat. fat), 3 mg chol., 120 mg sodium, 4 g carbo., 2 g pro.

green BEAN SALAD

Prep: 15 minutes
Chill: 1 hour
Makes: 6 servings

12 ounces fresh green beans, trimmed

8 ounces yellow and/or red cherry tomatoes, halved

½ of a small red onion, thinly sliced

Basil-Tomato Vinaigrette*

1 In a medium saucepan, cook green beans, covered, in a small amount of boiling lightly salted water for about 8 minutes or just until crisp-tender. Drain; rinse with cold water and drain again.

2 In a large bowl, combine beans, tomatoes, and red onion. Drizzle with Basil-Tomato Vinaigrette; toss gently to coat. Cover and chill for 1 to 4 hours.

*Basil-Tomato Vinaigrette: In a small bowl, stir together ⅓ cup snipped fresh basil; 3 tablespoons red wine vinegar; 2 tablespoons snipped dried tomatoes; 1 tablespoon olive oil; 2 cloves garlic, minced; ¼ teaspoon salt; and ¼ teaspoon ground black pepper.

Nutrition facts per serving: 53 cal., 2 g total fat (0 g sat. fat), 0 mg chol., 126 mg sodium, 8 g carbo., 2 g pro.

savory COUSCOUS

Add a garden-fresh note to any meal by jazzing up couscous with mushrooms, carrot, green onions, and basil or thyme.

Start to Finish: 20 minutes
Makes: 8 servings

- 2 cups water
- 1½ cups sliced fresh mushrooms
- ½ cup shredded carrot
- ⅓ cup thinly sliced green onions
- 1 tablespoon butter or margarine
- 2 teaspoons instant chicken bouillon granules
- ½ teaspoon dried basil or thyme, crushed
- 1 10-ounce package quick-cooking couscous

1 In a medium saucepan, combine the water, mushrooms, carrot, green onions, butter, bouillon granules, and basil or thyme; bring to boiling. Stir in couscous. Remove from heat.

2 Cover; let stand for about 5 minutes or until liquid is absorbed. Fluff with a fork before serving.

Nutrition facts per serving: 158 cal., 2 g total fat (1 g sat. fat), 4 mg chol., 241 mg sodium, 29 g carbo., 5 g pro.

bacon-onion BISCUITS

Prep: 30 minutes
Bake: 25 minutes
Oven: 350°F
Makes: 12 biscuits

4 slices bacon, chopped
1 large onion, chopped (1 cup)
3 cups all-purpose flour
1 tablespoon baking powder
1 tablespoon sugar
¾ teaspoon cream of tartar
½ teaspoon salt
¾ cup butter
1 cup milk

1 In a skillet, cook bacon and onion until bacon is slightly crisp and onion is tender. Drain and discard fat.

2 In a bowl, stir together flour, baking powder, sugar, cream of tartar, and salt. Using a pastry blender, cut in butter until mixture resembles coarse crumbs. Make a well in the center of flour mixture. Combine milk and bacon mixture; add all at once to flour mixture. Using a fork, stir just until moistened.

3 Turn dough out onto a lightly floured surface. Knead dough by folding and gently pressing dough for four to six strokes or just until dough holds together. Pat or lightly roll dough to ¾-inch thickness. Cut dough with a floured 2½-inch biscuit cutter, rerolling dough scraps as necessary. Place biscuits on a baking sheet; freeze for 1 hour. Transfer to a plastic freezer bag. Seal, label, and freeze for up to 1 month.

4 To serve, preheat oven to 350°F. Place frozen biscuits 1 inch apart on an ungreased baking sheet. Bake for 25 minutes or until golden.

Nutrition facts per biscuit: 294 cal., 18 g total fat (10 g sat. fat), 41 mg chol., 354 mg sodium, 27 g carbo., 6 g pro.

sweet
TREATS

Fresh Strawberry Fool, *recipe page 226*

berry PUDDING CAKES

Prep: 20 minutes
Bake: 20 minutes
Oven: 400°F
Makes: 6 servings

Nonstick cooking spray

2 **eggs, lightly beaten**

¼ **cup granulated sugar**

1 **teaspoon vanilla**

Pinch salt

1 **cup milk**

½ **cup all-purpose flour**

½ **teaspoon baking powder**

3 **cups fresh berries (such as raspberries, blueberries, and/or sliced strawberries)**

2 **teaspoons powdered sugar (optional)**

① Preheat oven to 400°F. Lightly coat six 6-ounce individual quiche dishes with nonstick cooking spray. Arrange in a 15×10×1-inch baking pan; set aside. In a medium bowl, combine eggs, granulated sugar, vanilla, and salt; whisk until light and frothy. Whisk in milk until combined. Add flour and baking powder; whisk until smooth.

② Divide berries among prepared quiche dishes. Pour batter over berries. (Batter will not cover berries completely.) Bake for about 20 minutes or until puffed and golden brown. Serve warm. If desired, sift powdered sugar over each serving.

Nutrition facts per serving: 149 cal., 3 g total fat (1 g sat. fat), 74 mg chol., 84 mg sodium, 26 g carbo., 5 g pro.

carrot SNACK CAKE

Usually you find carrot cake under a slathering of cream cheese frosting. Here powdered sugar steps in, cutting back on fat and calories.

Prep: 15 minutes
Bake: 30 minutes
Oven: 350°F
Makes: 12 servings

Nonstick cooking spray
1 **cup all-purpose flour**
¾ **cup granulated sugar**
1½ **teaspoons apple pie spice**
½ **teaspoon baking powder**
½ **teaspoon baking soda**
⅛ **teaspoon salt**
1 **cup finely shredded carrot**
⅓ **cup cooking oil**
¼ **cup low-fat milk**
3 **egg whites**
1 **teaspoon sifted powdered sugar**
Fresh raspberries (optional)

1 Preheat oven to 350°F. Lightly coat an 8x8x2-inch baking pan with nonstick cooking spray. Set aside.

2 In a large bowl, combine flour, granulated sugar, apple pie spice, baking powder, baking soda, and salt. Add carrot, oil, and milk. Stir to moisten. In a medium mixing bowl, beat egg whites with an electric mixer on medium to high speed until stiff peaks form (tips stand straight). Fold egg whites into carrot mixture.

3 Pour batter into the prepared pan. Bake for 30 to 35 minutes or until a wooden toothpick inserted near center comes out clean. Cool completely in pan on a wire rack.

4 To serve, dust with powdered sugar and, if desired, garnish with raspberries.

Nutrition facts per serving: 147 cal., 6 g total fat (1 g sat. fat), 0 mg chol., 114 mg sodium, 21 g carbo., 2 g pro.

mixed BERRY TRIFLE CAKES

Good things happen when the English trifle meets the all-American shortcake. Use any berries you like in this beautiful, bountiful dessert, but a combination of two or three kinds is best.

Start to Finish: 20 minutes
Makes: 8 servings

2 **4.5-ounce packages individual shortcake cups (8 cups)**

2 **tablespoons sugar-free apricot preserves**

2 **tablespoons orange juice**

1 **6-ounce carton fat-free vanilla yogurt with sweetener**

½ **teaspoon vanilla**

¼ **of an 8-ounce container frozen light whipped dessert topping, thawed**

1½ **cups mixed fresh berries (such as sliced strawberries, blueberries, raspberries, and/or blackberries)**

1 Arrange shortcake cups on a serving platter; set aside. In a small bowl, stir together preserves and orange juice. Spoon some of the mixture over each shortcake cup. In another small bowl, stir together yogurt and vanilla. Fold in whipped topping. Spoon yogurt mixture onto cake over preserves mixture. Top with berries.

Nutrition facts per serving: 153 cal., 3 g total fat (1 g sat. fat), 15 mg chol., 13 mg sodium, 28 g carbo., 2 g pro.

More Flavor

Fat-free, sugar-free yogurts are great multipurpose ingredients in healthy cooking. In addition to the flavor they provide, they add creaminess and moisture to recipes, both of which can be lost when fat is taken out. And, without much extra calories or fat, these yogurts add a protein and calcium boost. Vanilla and plain yogurts are neutral and mix well with any recipe, but why not get creative? Try a berry-flavor yogurt in this trifle recipe or coffee-flavor yogurt in a chocolate-based recipe.

warm CHOCOLATE BREAD PUDDING

Prep: 15 minutes
Bake: 15 minutes
Oven: 350°F
Makes: 4 servings

Nonstick cooking spray

2 cups firm-texture white bread cubes

⅔ cup milk

¼ cup granulated sugar

¼ cup miniature semisweet chocolate pieces

2 eggs

1 teaspoon finely shredded orange peel or tangerine peel

½ teaspoon vanilla

Frozen light whipped dessert topping or powdered sugar (optional)

1 Preheat oven to 350°F. Lightly coat four 6-ounce custard cups or ¾-cup soufflé dishes with cooking spray. Place bread cubes in the custard cups.

2 In a small saucepan, combine milk, granulated sugar, and chocolate. Cook and stir over low heat until chocolate melts; remove from heat. If necessary, beat smooth with a wire whisk.

3 In a medium bowl, beat eggs; gradually stir in chocolate mixture. Stir in orange peel and vanilla. Pour egg mixture over bread cubes; press bread with the back of a spoon to moisten.

4 Bake for 15 to 20 minutes or until tops appear firm and a knife inserted near the centers comes out clean. Cool slightly on a wire rack. If desired, top with whipped topping or dust with powdered sugar.

Nutrition facts per serving: 170 cal., 4 g total fat (2 g sat. fat), 1 mg chol., 143 mg sodium, 26 g carbo., 5 g pro.

double CHOCOLATE BROWNIES

Prep: 10 minutes
Bake: 15 minutes
Oven: 350°F
Makes: 16 brownies

Nonstick cooking spray

¼ **cup butter**

⅔ **cup granulated sugar**

½ **cup cold water**

1 **teaspoon vanilla**

1 **cup all-purpose flour**

¼ **cup unsweetened cocoa powder**

1 **teaspoon baking powder**

¼ **cup miniature semisweet chocolate pieces**

Powdered sugar

1 Preheat oven to 350°F. Lightly coat the bottom only of a 9×9x2-inch baking pan with nonstick cooking spray,

2 In a medium saucepan, melt butter; remove from heat. Stir in granulated sugar, the water, and vanilla. Stir in flour, cocoa powder, and baking powder until combined. Stir in miniature chocolate pieces. Pour batter into prepared pan.

3 Bake for 15 to 18 minutes or until a toothpick inserted near the center comes out clean. Cool on a wire rack. Remove from pan. Cut into bars. Dust with powdered sugar.

Nutrition facts per brownie: 113 cal., 4 g total fat (2 g sat. fat), 8 mg chol., 37 mg sodium, 17 g carbo., 1 g pro.

brownie BITES

These snack bites will do little harm to your waistline—especially if you share.

Prep: 12 minutes
Bake: 20 minutes
Cool: 1 hour
Oven: 350°F
Makes: 8 bars

2 **tablespoons butter**

⅓ **cup granulated sugar**

¼ **cup cold water**

½ **teaspoon vanilla**

½ **cup all-purpose flour**

2 **tablespoons unsweetened cocoa powder**

½ **teaspoon baking powder**

2 **tablespoons chopped walnuts or pecans**

Nonstick cooking spray

1 **teaspoon powdered sugar**

1 Preheat oven to 350°F. In a small saucepan, melt butter; remove from heat. Stir in granulated sugar, cold water, and vanilla. Stir in flour, cocoa powder, and baking powder until thoroughly combined. Stir in 1 tablespoon of the nuts.

2 Spray the bottom of an 8x4x2-inch loaf pan with nonstick cooking spray. Pour batter into pan. Sprinkle with remaining 1 tablespoon chopped nuts.

3 Bake for about 20 minutes or until a toothpick inserted near center comes out clean. Cool completely in pan on wire rack. Remove from pan. Cut into 8 bars. Dust with the powdered sugar.

Nutrition facts per bar: 104 cal., 4 g total fat (1 g sat. fat), 0 mg chol., 57 mg sodium, 15 g carbo., 1 g pro.

yo-yos

Like the toy, this goodie has two outsides with something in between: in this case, chocolate and sorbet. Play with different flavor options.

Prep: 30 minutes
Freeze: 1 hour
Makes: 12 cookie sandwiches

¼ **cup semisweet chocolate pieces**

¼ **teaspoon shortening**

24 **amaretti cookies (4.6 ounces total) or vanilla wafers**

⅓ **cup mango, orange, lemon, or raspberry sorbet**

1 In a heavy small saucepan, heat chocolate pieces and shortening over low heat just until melted. Cool slightly. Using a narrow metal spatula, spread about 1 teaspoon chocolate mixture on the flat side of half of the cookies. Place coated cookies, chocolate side up, on a wire rack until chocolate mixture is set.

2 Using a melon baller, place a small scoop of sorbet (about 1 rounded teaspoon) on top of the chocolate side of each coated cookie. Dip the melon baller into water between scoops to make the scoops come out neatly. Top sorbet with another cookie to make a sandwich. Cover and freeze for 1 to 4 hours.

Nutrition facts per cookie sandwich: 71 cal., 2 g total fat (0 g sat. fat), 6 mg chol., 7 mg sodium, 12 g carbo., 1 g pro.

spiced CORNMEAL COOKIES

These finger-shaped cookies contain cornmeal, which adds a bit of toasty crunch. Cinnamon and hazelnuts contribute spicy, sweet flavor, making these cookies the ultimate treat.

Prep: 30 minutes
Bake: 10 minutes
Makes: 24 cookies

¼ **cup margarine or butter**

¾ **cup all-purpose flour**

¼ **cup yellow cornmeal**

¼ **cup sugar**

1 **egg white**

¼ **teaspoon finely shredded lemon peel**

¼ **teaspoon vanilla**

⅛ **teaspoon salt**

⅛ **teaspoon ground cinnamon**

2 **tablespoons finely chopped hazelnuts or almonds**

1 Preheat oven to 375°F. In a large bowl, beat the margarine or butter with an electric mixer on medium to high speed for 30 seconds. Add about half of the flour, the cornmeal, sugar, egg white, lemon peel, vanilla, salt, and cinnamon. Beat until combined. Beat or stir in remaining flour. Stir in hazelnuts or almonds.

2 Shape the dough into 24 fingers about 2½ inches long. Place on an ungreased baking sheet. Bake for about 10 minutes or until the bottoms are golden. Transfer to a wire rack; cool.

Nutrition facts per cookie: 48 cal., 2 g total fat (0 g sat. fat), 0 mg chol., 36 mg sodium, 6 g carbo., 1 g pro.

chocolate-mint COOKIES

Kids eagerly accept these fudgy treats as an after-school snack along with a cold glass of milk.

Prep: 30 minutes
Freeze: 30 minutes
Bake: 9 minutes per batch
Oven: 350°F
Makes: about 36 cookies

1⅓ **cups all-purpose flour**

1 **cup no-calorie, heat-stable granular sugar substitute**

1½ **teaspoons baking powder**

¼ **teaspoon salt**

1 **cup semisweet chocolate pieces**

⅓ **cup butter, softened**

2 **eggs**

1½ **teaspoons vanilla**

¼ **teaspoon mint extract**

Powdered sugar (optional)

1 Preheat oven to 350°F. In a bowl, combine flour, sugar substitute, baking powder, and salt; set aside.

2 In a small saucepan, heat chocolate pieces over low heat until melted, stirring constantly.

3 In a large mixing bowl, beat butter with an electric mixer on high speed for 1 minute. Beat in melted chocolate, eggs, vanilla, and mint extract.

4 Gradually beat in flour mixture. Wrap dough in plastic wrap. Freeze for 30 minutes or until firm enough to shape into balls. Shape dough into 1-inch balls. Place balls about 1½ inches apart on an ungreased cookie sheet. Bake for 9 to 11 minutes or until tops are cracked. Transfer cookies to a wire rack; cool.

5 If desired, dust cookies lightly with powdered sugar before serving. Store for up to 2 days at room temperature. Freeze for longer storage.

Nutrition facts per cookie: 63 cal., 4 g total fat (2 g sat. fat), 17 mg chol., 56 mg sodium, 7 g carbo., 1 g pro.

salted PEANUT BARS

Prep: 25 minutes
Chill: 1 hour
Makes: 60 pieces

Nonstick cooking spray

4 **cups dry-roasted or honey-roasted peanuts**

1 **10.5-ounce package tiny marshmallows**

½ **cup butter**

1 **14-ounce can sweetened condensed milk (1⅓ cups)**

1 **10-ounce package peanut butter–flavor pieces**

½ **cup creamy peanut butter**

1 Line a 13x9x2-inch baking pan with heavy foil. Coat foil with nonstick cooking spray. Spread half of the peanuts evenly in prepared baking pan.

2 In a 3-quart saucepan, combine marshmallows and butter; heat and stir over medium-low heat until melted. Stir in sweetened condensed milk, peanut butter pieces, and peanut butter until smooth. Quickly pour peanut butter mixture over peanuts in pan. Sprinkle remaining peanuts over peanut butter mixture. Gently press peanuts into peanut butter mixture.

3 Chill for about 1 hour or until firm; cut into pieces. Store, covered, in refrigerator.

Nutrition facts per piece: 144 cal., 10 g total fat (3 g sat. fat), 7 mg chol., 128 mg sodium, 12 g carbo., 4 g pro.

apple AND PEANUT BUTTER CRISP

Prep: 20 minutes
Bake: 30 minutes
Oven: 375°F
Makes: 8 servings

6 medium red and/or green
   cooking apples, cored,
   peeled if desired, and thinly
   sliced

2 tablespoons all-purpose flour

1 tablespoon brown sugar

⅔ cup quick-cooking rolled oats

2 tablespoons all-purpose flour

2 tablespoons brown sugar

¼ cup peanut butter

2 tablespoons chopped peanuts

1 Preheat oven to 375°F. Place apple slices in a 2-quart square baking dish. In a small bowl, stir together 2 tablespoons flour and 1 tablespoon brown sugar until well combined. Sprinkle over apple slices in dish; toss to coat.

2 Bake, covered, for 15 minutes. Meanwhile, in a medium bowl, combine rolled oats, 2 tablespoons flour, and 2 tablespoons brown sugar. Using a fork, stir in peanut butter until mixture resembles coarse crumbs. Stir in peanuts.

3 Uncover apple mixture; sprinkle with oat mixture. Bake, uncovered, for 15 to 20 minutes more or until apples are tender and topping is golden. Serve warm.

Nutrition facts per serving: 174 cal., 6 g total fat (1 g sat. fat), 0 mg chol., 51 mg sodium, 28 g carbo., 4 g pro.

apple-CRANBERRY CRISP

As tasty as it is simple to fix, this down-home recipe will remind you of one of your Grandma's old-fashioned autumn desserts.

Prep: 15 minutes
Bake: 30 minutes
Oven: 375°F
Makes: 6 servings

5 cups thinly sliced peeled apples

1 cup cranberries

2 tablespoons granulated sugar

½ teaspoon apple pie spice or ground cinnamon

½ cup quick-cooking rolled oats

3 tablespoons packed brown sugar

2 tablespoons all-purpose flour

½ teaspoon apple pie spice or ground cinnamon

2 tablespoons butter

1 Preheat oven to 375°F. In a 2-quart baking dish, combine apples and cranberries. Stir together granulated sugar and ½ teaspoon apple pie spice. Sprinkle over fruit mixture in dish; toss to coat.

2 In a small bowl, combine oats, brown sugar, flour, and ½ teaspoon apple pie spice. Cut in butter until crumbly. Sprinkle oat mixture evenly over apple mixture.

3 Bake for 30 to 35 minutes or until apples are tender. Serve warm.

Nutrition facts per serving: 189 cal., 5 g total fat (3 g sat. fat), 11 mg chol., 45 mg sodium, 37 g carbo., 2 g pro.

raspberry-peach CRISP

Prep: 30 minutes
Bake: 45 minutes
Cool: 45 minutes
Oven: 375°F
Makes: 8 servings

4 cups sliced fresh peaches or
   frozen unsweetened peach
   slices, thawed

2 tablespoons granulated sugar

1 tablespoon quick-cooking
   tapioca

2 tablespoons red raspberry
   preserves

⅔ cup quick-cooking rolled oats

2 tablespoons whole wheat
   flour

2 tablespoons packed brown
   sugar

½ teaspoon ground cinnamon

2 tablespoons butter

   Low-fat vanilla yogurt
   or vanilla frozen yogurt
   (optional)

1 Preheat oven to 375°F. For fruit filling, thaw fruit, if frozen; do not drain. In a large bowl, combine peach slices, granulated sugar, tapioca, and raspberry preserves. Place fruit mixture in a 2-quart square baking dish.

2 For the topping, in a medium bowl, combine oats, whole wheat flour, brown sugar, and cinnamon. Using a pastry blender, cut in butter until crumbly. Sprinkle topping over fruit.

3 Bake for 45 to 50 minutes or until bubbly. Cool on a wire rack for 45 minutes; serve warm. If desired, serve with vanilla yogurt.

Nutrition facts per serving: 159 cal., 4 g total fat (2 g sat. fat), 8 mg chol., 22 mg sodium, 31 g carbo., 3 g pro.

peach-berry COBBLER

Cobbler is the ultimate comfort food. You'll agree when you spoon into syrupy peaches and raspberries covered with spicy biscuit topping, served hot with a scoop of low-fat vanilla ice cream.

Prep: 30 minutes
Cook: 25 minutes
Makes: 8 servings

- **4 cups fresh or frozen unsweetened peach slices, thawed**
- **¼ cup sugar**
- **¼ cup water**
- **4 teaspoons cornstarch**
- **1 tablespoon lemon juice**
- **¼ teaspoon ground allspice or ground cardamom**
- **Biscuit Topping***
- **1½ cups fresh raspberries or frozen raspberries, thawed**

① Preheat oven to 400°F. For filling, in a medium saucepan combine the peaches, 2 tablespoons of the sugar, the water, cornstarch, lemon juice, and allspice or cardamom. Let stand for 10 minutes.

② Meanwhile, prepare Biscuit Topping.

③ Cook and stir the peach mixture over medium heat until thickened and bubbly. Stir in the raspberries. Transfer the hot filling to a 2-quart square baking dish.

④ Immediately drop the Biscuit Topping into 8 small mounds on the hot filling. Sprinkle topping with the remaining sugar.

⑤ Bake for about 25 minutes or until a toothpick inserted into topping comes out clean.

***Biscuit Topping:** In a large bowl, combine 1¼ cups all-purpose flour, 2 tablespoons sugar, ¾ teaspoon baking powder, ¼ teaspoon baking soda, ¼ teaspoon ground allspice or ground cardamom, and ⅛ teaspoon salt. In a small bowl, stir together ½ cup fat-free lemon or plain yogurt; ¼ cup refrigerated or frozen egg substitute, thawed, or 1 large beaten egg; and 2 tablespoons melted butter or margarine. Add egg mixture to flour mixture, stirring just to moisten.

Nutrition facts per serving: 202 cal., 4 g total fat (2 g sat. fat), 8 mg chol., 159 mg sodium, 40 g carbo., 4 g pro.

caramel APPLE PASTRY

Refrigerated piecrust is a dessert lover's best friend. It's versatile, convenient, and—best of all—tastes wonderful, especially when paired with sliced apples and brown sugar.

Prep: 10 minutes
Bake: 15 minutes
Cool: 5 minutes
Oven: 450°F
Makes: 6 servings

½ of a 15-ounce package (1 crust) rolled refrigerated unbaked piecrust

1 tablespoon butter

2 20-ounce cans sliced apples, well drained

½ cup packed brown sugar

1 tablespoon lemon juice

1 teaspoon apple pie spice or ground cinnamon

1 tablespoon purchased cinnamon-sugar

Cinnamon or vanilla ice cream (optional)

Caramel ice cream topping (optional)

1 Preheat oven to 450°F. Bring piecrust to room temperature in microwave oven according to package directions; set aside. In a large ovenproof skillet, melt butter over high heat; stir in drained apple slices, brown sugar, lemon juice, and apple pie spice. Spread evenly in skillet. Cook until bubbly.

2 Meanwhile, on a lightly floured surface, unroll piecrust. Sprinkle piecrust with cinnamon-sugar; rub into crust with your fingers. Carefully place piecrust, cinnamon-sugar side up, over bubbly apple mixture in skillet. Tuck in piecrust around edge of skillet, using a spatula to press edge down slightly.

3 Bake for about 15 minutes or until piecrust is golden brown. Cool for 5 minutes. Carefully invert skillet onto a serving platter; remove skillet. Serve warm. If desired, serve with ice cream and caramel topping.

Nutrition facts per serving: 381 cal., 12 g total fat (5 g sat. fat), 12 mg chol., 159 mg sodium, 69 g carbo., 1 g pro.

maple-nut BAKED APPLES

These apples are pleasers alone or topped with frozen yogurt.

Prep: 15 minutes
Bake: 25 minutes
Oven: 350°F
Makes: 4 servings

- 2 **medium cooking apples, such as Rome Beauty, Granny Smith, or Jonathan**
- 3 **tablespoons water**
- 3 **tablespoons sugar-free maple-flavor syrup with no-calorie, heat-stable granular sugar substitute**
- ¼ **cup snipped dried figs, snipped pitted whole dates, raisins, or mixed dried fruit bits**
- ¼ **teaspoon apple pie spice or ground cinnamon**
- 2 **tablespoons chopped toasted pecans or walnuts**

    Low-fat vanilla frozen yogurt (optional)

1 Preheat oven to 350°F. Core apples; peel a strip from the top of each. In a 2-quart square baking dish, stir together the water and 2 tablespoons of the maple-flavor syrup. Add apples to dish. In a small bowl, combine dried fruit, remaining 1 tablespoon syrup, and apple pie spice; spoon into center of apples. Cover dish with foil; fold back one corner of foil to vent. Bake for 25 to 30 minutes or until the apples are tender, spooning syrup mixture over apples once halfway through baking.

2 To serve, halve warm apples lengthwise. Transfer apple halves to dessert dishes. Spoon some of the cooking liquid over apples. Sprinkle with nuts. If desired, top with a small scoop of frozen yogurt.

Nutrition facts per serving: 103 cal., 3 g total fat (1 g sat. fat), 0 mg chol., 21 mg sodium, 22 g carbo., 1 g pro.

Healthy Holiday Eating

The challenge of healthy eating grows more difficult during the holidays, when high-fat, sugar-laden foods are everywhere. Keeping the principles of a healthy lifestyle at the forefront is especially important. In addition to sticking with your exercise routine, continue to eat scheduled meals. Eating regularly keeps you from getting hungry and makes it easier to say no. When faced with something you can't or don't want to say no to, find a way to make it fit into your meal plan. Try eating a small amount with a meal or eating just a little bit less of everything to make room for the extra calories.

pumpkin-maple PIE

It tastes like Grandmother's, but it's better for you! Our special lower-fat pastry is filled with a maple-flavored pumpkin mixture that is lower in calories and fat than old-fashioned recipes—but it is every bit as good!

Prep: 25 minutes
Bake: 45 minutes
Makes: 8 servings

Lower-Fat Oil Pastry*

1 **15-ounce can pumpkin**

⅓ **cup maple-flavored syrup**

1 **tablespoon all-purpose flour**

2 **packets heat-stable granular sugar substitute**

1½ **teaspoons pumpkin pie spice**

¾ **cup refrigerated or frozen egg product, thawed**

1 **cup evaporated fat-free milk**

1½ **teaspoons vanilla**

Frozen light whipped dessert topping, thawed (optional)

1 Preheat oven to 375°F. Prepare Lower-Fat Oil Pastry. On a lightly floured surface, flatten pastry. Roll into a 12-inch circle. Wrap pastry circle around the rolling pin; unroll into a 9-inch pie plate. Ease pastry into pan, being careful not to stretch pastry. Trim to ½ inch beyond edge of pie plate. Fold under extra pastry. Crimp the edge as desired. Do not prick pastry.

2 For the filling, in a medium bowl combine the pumpkin, maple-flavored syrup, flour, sugar substitute, and pumpkin pie spice; add egg product. Beat lightly with a rotary beater or fork until just combined. Gradually stir in evaporated milk and vanilla; mix well.

3 Place pastry-lined pie plate on oven rack. Carefully pour filling into pastry shell. To prevent overbrowning, cover edge of pie with foil. Bake for 25 minutes. Remove the foil. Bake for 20 to 25 minutes more or until a knife inserted near the center comes out clean. Cool on a wire rack. Cover and refrigerate within 2 hours. If desired, serve with whipped dessert topping.

*Lower-Fat Oil Pastry: In a medium bowl, stir together 1¼ cups all-purpose flour and ¼ teaspoon salt. Combine ¼ cup fat-free milk and 3 tablespoons cooking oil; add all at once to flour mixture. Stir with a fork until dough forms. If necessary, add 1 to 2 teaspoons additional milk. Shape the dough into a ball.

Nutrition facts per serving: 216 cal., 6 g total fat (1 g sat. fat), 1 mg chol., 153 mg sodium, 32 g carbo., 8 g pro.

pumpkin-pear CAKE

Prep: 25 minutes
Bake: 35 minutes
Cool: 35 minutes
Makes: 16 servings

1 cup packed brown sugar

⅓ cup butter, melted

1½ teaspoons cornstarch

2 15-ounce cans pear halves in light syrup

½ cup coarsely chopped pecans

1 2-layer-size spice cake mix

1 cup canned pumpkin

① Preheat oven to 350°F. In a small bowl, stir together brown sugar, butter, and cornstarch. Drain pears, reserving 3 tablespoons of the syrup. Stir reserved syrup into brown sugar mixture. Pour mixture into a 13×9×2-inch baking pan. If desired, cut pear halves into fans by making 3 or 4 lengthwise cuts ¼ inch from the stem end of each pear half to the bottom of the pear half. Arrange pear halves on top of syrup in pan, cored sides down. Sprinkle pecans evenly into pan.

② Prepare cake mix according to package directions, except decrease oil to 2 tablespoons and add pumpkin. Slowly pour cake batter into pan, spreading evenly.

③ Bake for 35 to 40 minutes or until a wooden toothpick inserted near the center comes out clean. Cool in pan on a wire rack for 5 minutes. Run a thin metal spatula around edges of cake. Carefully invert cake into a 15×10×1-inch baking pan or onto a very large serving platter with slightly raised sides. Cool for about 30 minutes before serving. Serve warm.

Nutrition facts per serving: 337 cal., 15 g total fat (4 g sat. fat), 51 mg chol., 254 mg sodium, 51 g carbo., 3 g pro.

cinnamon-glazed POACHED PEARS

Prep: 20 minutes
Cook: 50 minutes
Cool: 30 minutes
Chill: 2 hours
Makes: 4 servings

4 **medium Bartlett pears**

1½ **cups pomegranate or cranberry juice**

1 **cup water**

2 **tablespoons honey**

6 **inches stick cinnamon or ¼ teaspoon ground cinnamon**

1 Cut a thin slice from the bottom of each pear so pears stand up. If desired, use a melon baller to remove the core through the bottom of each pear.

2 In a large saucepan, combine juice, the water, honey, and cinnamon. Bring to boiling, stirring to dissolve honey. Add pears. Return to boiling; reduce heat. Cook, covered, for about 10 minutes or just until pears are tender. Remove pan from heat and let cool for 30 minutes. Transfer pears and liquid to a large bowl, turning pears a few times to coat with liquid. Cover and chill for 2 to 24 hours.

3 Remove pears from liquid; cover and chill until ready to serve or, if desired, pears may stand at room temperature while syrup is being reduced. Strain liquid; discard stick cinnamon, if using. Transfer liquid to a medium saucepan. Bring to boiling; simmer gently, uncovered, for about 40 minutes or until reduced to ¼ cup. Watch mixture closely at the end to prevent overcooking. To serve, drizzle reduced liquid over pears.

Nutrition facts per serving: 177 cal., 0 g total fat, 0 mg chol., 16 mg sodium, 47 g carbo., 1 g pro.

fruit PARFAIT

Parfait, in French, means "perfect," which is what you'll think of this dessert. Served in tall parfait glasses, the layers of fruit and cream look striking, especially when sprinkled with grated chocolate.

Prep: 20 minutes
Makes: 4 servings

½ cup fat-free dairy sour cream

Low-calorie powdered sweetener equal to 1½ teaspoons sugar, or 1 tablespoon powdered sugar

1 tablespoon orange liqueur, raspberry liqueur, melon liqueur, or orange juice

¼ of an 8-ounce container frozen light whipped dessert topping, thawed

1½ cups sliced, peeled peaches

1 cup raspberries

1 cup blueberries

Grated chocolate (optional)

1 In a medium bowl, stir together the sour cream, powdered sweetener or powdered sugar, and liqueur or orange juice. Gently fold in dessert topping.

2 In four parfait glasses, layer half of the peaches, raspberries, blueberries, and sour cream mixture. Repeat layering. If desired, sprinkle grated chocolate over each serving. Serve parfaits immediately or cover and chill for up to 2 hours.

Nutrition facts per serving: 134 cal., 2 g total fat (2 g sat. fat), 0 mg chol., 33 mg sodium, 25 g carbo., 3 g pro.

nectarine TART

The filling in this low-fat dessert tastes deceivingly rich. Fat-free cream cheese is the key. For a pretty finish, arrange the nectarines or peaches and blueberries in a pinwheel design before adding the apricot spread.

Prep: 35 minutes
Bake: 12 minutes
Chill: 2 hours
Makes: 12 servings

- **1 cup all-purpose flour**
- **¼ teaspoon salt**
- **¼ cup margarine or butter**
- **4 to 5 tablespoons cold water**
- **1 8-ounce package fat-free cream cheese, softened**
- **Sugar substitute equal to ¼ cup sugar, or ¼ cup sugar**
- **1 teaspoon vanilla**
- **4 or 5 nectarines or peeled peaches, pitted and sliced, or one 16-ounce package frozen unsweetened peach slices, thawed and drained**
- **½ cup blueberries**
- **½ cup low-calorie apricot spread**

1 Preheat oven to 450°F. For pastry, in a medium bowl combine flour and salt. Using a pastry blender, cut in margarine or butter until pieces are the size of small peas. Sprinkle 1 tablespoon of the cold water over a portion of the mixture. Toss with a fork. Push to side of bowl. Repeat until mixture is moistened. Form into a ball.

2 On a lightly floured surface, flatten pastry. Roll pastry into a 12-inch circle. Ease pastry into a 10-inch tart pan with a removable bottom, being careful not to stretch pastry. Press pastry about ½ inch up the sides of pan. Prick the bottom well with the tines of a fork. Bake for 12 to 15 minutes or until golden. Cool on a wire rack. Remove sides of tart pan.

3 Meanwhile, in a medium bowl combine the cream cheese, sugar substitute or sugar, and vanilla. Beat with an electric mixer until smooth; spread over the cooled pastry. Arrange the nectarines or peaches over cream cheese layer. Sprinkle with the blueberries.

4 In a small saucepan, heat apricot spread until melted; cut up any large pieces. Spoon melted spread over fruit. Chill for at least 2 hours or up to 3 hours.

Nutrition facts per serving: 140 cal., 4 g total fat (1 g sat. fat), 3 mg chol., 90 mg sodium, 23 g carbo., 4 g pro.

berry-ginger SHORTCAKES

Like classic shortcakes, but better! These sweet biscuits are split in half, filled with low-calorie sweetened berries, and topped with sour cream–flavored whipped topping. Heavenly!

Prep: 25 minutes
Bake: 8 minutes
Makes: 10 servings

3 cups berries (such as sliced strawberries, blueberries, raspberries, and/or blackberries)

Low-calorie liquid sweetener equal to 2 tablespoons sugar (optional)

2 tablespoons finely chopped crystallized ginger

Shortcakes*

½ of an 8-ounce container frozen fat-free whipped dessert topping, thawed

¼ cup fat-free dairy sour cream

1 In a small mixing bowl combine the berries, the liquid sweetener (if desired), and the crystallized ginger. Set aside.

2 Meanwhile, prepare Shortcakes.

3 To serve, in a small bowl combine the whipped topping and sour cream. Split shortcakes in half. Place bottoms on dessert plates. Divide the berry mixture among bottoms. Top each with some of the whipped topping mixture. Replace the shortcake tops.

*Shortcakes: In a medium bowl, stir together 1⅔ cups all-purpose flour, 1 tablespoon sugar, 2 teaspoons baking powder, and ¼ teaspoon baking soda. Using a pastry blender, cut in 3 tablespoons butter or margarine until the mixture resembles coarse crumbs. Combine ½ cup buttermilk and ¼ cup refrigerated or frozen egg product (thawed) or 1 egg. Add to the flour mixture all at once, stirring just until mixture is moistened. Spray a baking sheet with nonstick coating. On a lightly floured surface, pat the dough to ½-inch thickness. Cut the dough with a floured 2½-inch star-shaped or heart-shaped cookie cutter or a round biscuit cutter, rerolling scraps as necessary. Place shortcakes on prepared baking sheet. Bake in a 425°F oven for 8 to 10 minutes or until golden. Cool the shortcakes slightly on a wire rack.

Nutrition facts per serving: 166 cal., 4 g total fat (2 g sat. fat), 10 mg chol., 176 mg sodium, 28 g carbo., 4 g pro.

fresh STRAWBERRY FOOL

Fresh berries and a luscious yogurt whipped cream make a simple yet elegant classic English dessert. Crumbled cookies add delightful crunch.

Start to Finish: 15 minutes
Makes: 4 servings

½ cup whipping cream

⅓ cup powdered sugar

½ teaspoon vanilla

1 8-ounce carton low-fat lemon yogurt

3 cups sliced fresh strawberries or 2 cups fresh blueberries

½ cup coarsely crumbled shortbread cookies (5 cookies)

1 In a chilled medium bowl, combine whipping cream, powdered sugar, and vanilla. Beat with chilled beaters of an electric mixer on medium speed or a chilled rotary beater until soft peaks form (tips curl). By hand, fold in the yogurt.

2 Spoon the whipped cream mixture into four dessert dishes. Top with berries. Sprinkle with the crumbled cookies.

Make Ahead: Prepare as directed, except do not sprinkle with crumbled cookies. Cover and chill for up to 2 hours. To serve, sprinkle with crumbled cookies.

Nutrition facts per serving: 272 cal., 15 g total fat (8 g sat. fat), 47 mg chol., 98 mg sodium, 32 g carbo., 4 g pro.

tiramisu CUPS

This lightened version of the popular Italian dessert is a snap to make at home.

Prep: 20 minutes
Chill: 1 hour
Makes: 4 servings

½ of a 3-ounce package
  ladyfingers, cubed
  (12 halves)

¼ cup espresso or strong coffee

¼ of an 8-ounce package
  reduced-fat cream cheese
  (Neufchâtel), softened

½ cup light dairy sour cream

  Sugar substitute to equal
  3 tablespoons sugar

1 teaspoon vanilla

½ teaspoon unsweetened cocoa
  powder

1 Divide half of the ladyfinger cubes among four 4- to 6-ounce dessert dishes. Drizzle ladyfinger cubes with half of the espresso. Set aside.

2 In a medium bowl, stir cream cheese to soften. Stir in sour cream, sugar substitute, and vanilla. (Beat smooth with a wire whisk, if necessary.) Spoon half of the cream cheese mixture over ladyfinger cubes. Add remaining ladyfinger cubes and drizzle with remaining espresso. Cover and chill for 1 to 24 hours. Just before serving, top with remaining cream cheese mixture and sprinkle with cocoa powder.

Nutrition facts per serving: 124 cal., 8 g total fat (5 g sat. fat), 61 mg chol., 85 mg sodium, 9 g carbo., 3 g pro.

berry CHEESECAKE DESSERT

Fat-free cream cheese and low-fat ricotta cheese lend rich taste to this cheesecake. Serve it when fresh berries are in season, as a tempting finale to a festive dinner.

Prep: 20 minutes
Chill: 4 to 24 hours
Makes: 4 servings

½ of an 8-ounce tub (about ½ cup) fat-free cream cheese

½ cup low-fat ricotta cheese

Low-calorie powdered sweetener equal to 3 tablespoons sugar, or 3 tablespoons sugar

½ teaspoon finely shredded orange peel or lemon peel

1 tablespoon orange juice

3 cups sliced strawberries, raspberries, and/or blueberries

4 gingersnaps or chocolate wafers, broken

1 In a blender container or food processor bowl, combine cream cheese, ricotta cheese, powdered sweetener or sugar, orange or lemon peel, and orange juice. Cover and blend or process until smooth. Cover and chill for 4 to 24 hours.

2 To serve, divide the fruit among dessert dishes. Top each serving with the cream cheese mixture and sprinkle with the broken cookies.

Nutrition facts per serving: 115 cal., 2 g total fat (1 g sat. fat), 9 mg chol., 61 mg sodium, 17 g carbo., 8 g pro.

peaches AND ICE CREAM SANDWICH BARS

Prep: 25 minutes
Freeze: 4¼ hours
Stand: 10 minutes
Makes: 12 servings

10 to 14 rectangular ice cream
    sandwiches
 2 pints peach or mango sorbet,
    softened
 1 8-ounce carton dairy sour
    cream
 1 cup whipping cream
 ¾ cup sifted powdered sugar
 2 cups fresh blueberries or
    raspberries

1 Place ice cream sandwiches in a 13×9×2-inch baking pan or 3-quart rectangular baking dish, cutting to fit. Spread sorbet on top of ice cream sandwiches. Cover and freeze for 15 minutes or until sorbet is firm.

2 In a medium bowl, combine sour cream, whipping cream, and powdered sugar. Beat with electric mixer on medium speed until mixture thickens and holds soft peaks. Spread on top of sorbet.

3 Cover and freeze for 4 to 24 hours or until firm. Let stand at room temperature for 10 minutes before serving. Sprinkle fresh berries over whipped cream mixture.

Nutrition facts per serving: 354 cal., 16 g total fat (10 g sat. fat), 52 mg chol., 49 mg sodium, 51 g carbo., 3 g pro.

raspberry CHEESECAKE SHAKES

Start to Finish: 10 minutes
Makes: 6 servings

1　**12-ounce package frozen unsweetened red raspberries, thawed**

1　**3-ounce package cream cheese, softened**

¼　**teaspoon almond extract**

1　**quart vanilla ice cream, softened**

2　**12-ounce cans or bottles cream soda**

　Fresh raspberries (optional)

1 In a blender, combine raspberries, cream cheese, and almond extract; add half of the ice cream and ½ cup of the cream soda. Cover and blend until smooth.

2 Pour into six 16-ounce glasses. Add a scoop of the remaining ice cream to each glass. Top with remaining cream soda.

3 If desired, garnish with fresh raspberries. Serve immediately.

Nutrition facts per serving: 305 cal., 15 g total fat (9 g sat. fat), 54 mg chol., 130 mg sodium, 36 g carbo., 4 g pro.

metric information

The charts on this page provide a guide for converting measurements from the U.S. customary system, which is used throughout this book, to the metric system.

PRODUCT DIFFERENCES

Most of the ingredients called for in the recipes in this book are available in most countries. However, some are known by different names. Here are some common American ingredients and their possible counterparts:

- Sugar (white) is granulated, fine granulated, or castor sugar.
- Powdered sugar is icing sugar.
- All-purpose flour is enriched, bleached, or unbleached white household flour. When self-rising flour is used in place of all-purpose flour in a recipe that calls for leavening, omit the leavening agent (baking soda or baking powder) and salt.
- Light-colored corn syrup is golden syrup.
- Cornstarch is cornflour.
- Baking soda is bicarbonate of soda.
- Vanilla or vanilla extract is vanilla essence.
- Green, red, or yellow sweet peppers are capsicums or bell peppers.
- Golden raisins are sultanas.

VOLUME AND WEIGHT

The United States traditionally uses cup measures for liquid and solid ingredients. The chart, top right, shows the approximate imperial and metric equivalents. If you are accustomed to weighing solid ingredients, the following approximate equivalents will be helpful.

- 1 cup butter, castor sugar, or rice = 8 ounces = $1/2$ pound = 250 grams
- 1 cup flour = 4 ounces = $1/4$ pound = 125 grams
- 1 cup icing sugar = 5 ounces = 150 grams

Canadian and U.S. volume for a cup measure is 8 fluid ounces (237 ml), but the standard metric equivalent is 250 ml.

1 British imperial cup is 10 fluid ounces.

In Australia, 1 tablespoon equals 20 ml, and there are 4 teaspoons in the Australian tablespoon.

Spoon measures are used for smaller amounts of ingredients. Although the size of the tablespoon varies slightly in different countries, for practical purposes and for recipes in this book, a straight substitution is all that's necessary. Measurements made using cups or spoons always should be level unless stated otherwise.

COMMON WEIGHT RANGE REPLACEMENTS

Imperial / U.S.	Metric
$1/2$ ounce	15 g
1 ounce	25 g or 30 g
4 ounces ($1/4$ pound)	115 g or 125 g
8 ounces ($1/2$ pound)	225 g or 250 g
16 ounces (1 pound)	450 g or 500 g
$1^1/4$ pounds	625 g
$1^1/2$ pounds	750 g
2 pounds or $2^1/4$ pounds	1,000 g or 1 Kg

OVEN TEMPERATURE EQUIVALENTS

Fahrenheit Setting	Celsius Setting*	Gas Setting
300°F	150°C	Gas Mark 2 (very low)
325°F	160°C	Gas Mark 3 (low)
350°F	180°C	Gas Mark 4 (moderate)
375°F	190°C	Gas Mark 5 (moderate)
400°F	200°C	Gas Mark 6 (hot)
425°F	220°C	Gas Mark 7 (hot)
450°F	230°C	Gas Mark 8 (very hot)
475°F	240°C	Gas Mark 9 (very hot)
500°F	260°C	Gas Mark 10 (extremely hot)
Broil	Broil	Grill

*Electric and gas ovens may be calibrated using Celsius. However, for an electric oven, increase Celsius setting 10 to 20 degrees when cooking above 160°C. For convection or forced air ovens (gas or electric), lower the temperature setting 25°F/10°C when cooking at all heat levels.

BAKING PAN SIZES

Imperial / U.S.	Metric
9×$1^1/2$-inch round cake pan	22- or 23×4-cm (1.5 L)
9×$1^1/2$-inch pie plate	22- or 23×4-cm (1 L)
8×8×2-inch square cake pan	20×5-cm (2 L)
9×9×2-inch square cake pan	22- or 23×4.5-cm (2.5 L)
11×7×$1^1/2$-inch baking pan	28×17×4-cm (2 L)
2-quart rectangular baking pan	30×19×4.5-cm (3 L)
13×9×2-inch baking pan	34×22×4.5-cm (3.5 L)
15×10×1-inch jelly roll pan	40×25×2-cm
9×5×3-inch loaf pan	23×13×8-cm (2 L)
2-quart casserole	2 L

U.S. / STANDARD METRIC EQUIVALENTS

$1/8$ teaspoon = 0.5 ml	$1/3$ cup = 3 fluid ounces = 75 ml
$1/4$ teaspoon = 1 ml	$1/2$ cup = 4 fluid ounces = 125 ml
$1/2$ teaspoon = 2 ml	$1/3$ cup = 5 fluid ounces = 150 ml
1 teaspoon = 5 ml	$3/4$ cup = 6 fluid ounces = 175 ml
1 tablespoon = 15 ml	1 cup = 8 fluid ounces = 250 ml
2 tablespoons = 25 ml	2 cups = 1 pint = 500 ml
$1/4$ cup = 2 fluid ounces = 50 ml	1 quart = 1 liter

index

Note: *Italicized* page references indicate photographs.